MICK JAGGER

THE UNAUTHORISED BIOGRAPHY

Printed in the United Kingdom by MPG Books, Bodmin

Published by Sanctuary Publishing Limited, Sanctuary House, 45-53 Sinclair Road, London W14 0NS, United Kingdom

www.sanctuarypublishing.com

Distributed in the US by Publishers Group West

ISBN: 1-86074-613-6

A L A N   C L A Y S O N

MICKJAGGER

THE UNAUTHORISED BIOGRAPHY

Sanctuary

To Kevin Delaney

'I don't take anything seriously. Since the age of 14, I haven't taken anything really seriously, whatever I do.'

Mick Jagger

Contents

About The Author

Born in Dover, England, in 1951, Alan Clayson lives near Henley-on-Thames with his wife, Inese. Their sons, Jack and Harry, are both at university.

A portrayal of Alan Clayson by the *Western Morning News* as the 'AJP Taylor of the pop world' is supported by *Q*'s 'his knowledge of the period is unparalleled and he's always unerringly accurate'. He has penned many books on music – including the best-sellers *Backbeat* (subject of a major film), *The Yardbirds* and *The Beatles Box* – and has written for journals as diverse as *The Guardian*, *Record Collector*, *Ink*, *Mojo*, *Mediaeval World*, *Folk Roots*, *Guitar*, *Hello!*, *Drummer*, *The Times*, *The Independent*, *Ugly Things* and, as a teenager, the notorious *Schoolkids Oz*. He has also been engaged to perform and lecture on both sides of the Atlantic, as well as broadcast on national TV and radio.

From 1975 to 1985, he led the legendary Clayson and the Argonauts, and was thrust to 'a premier position on rock's Lunatic Fringe' (*Melody Maker*). As shown by the existence of a US fan club – dating from a 1992 *soirée* in Chicago – Alan's following grows still, as does demand for his talents as a record producer and the number of versions of his compositions by such diverse acts as Dave Berry (for whom he played keyboards in the mid-1980s) and new-age outfit Stairway. He has also worked with The Portsmouth Sinfonia, Wreckless Eric, Twinkle, The Yardbirds, The Pretty Things and the late Screaming Lord Sutch, among many others. While his stage act defies succinct description, he has been labelled a 'chansonnier' in recent years for performances and record releases that may stand collectively as Alan Clayson's artistic apotheosis, were it not for a promise of surprises yet to come.

Further information is obtainable from www.alanclayson.com.

Prologue
Big Boss Man

'He's the best pop performer Britain's ever had. Without Mick, the Stones would have been nothing.'

– *Brian Jones*[1]

In the end, Brian Jones may have been reluctant to praise the deeds and character of one who, with Keith Richards, usurped his position as the artistic and aesthetic pivot of The Rolling Stones. The Elvis of the Swinging '60s and beyond, Mick Jagger will always be an object of fascination – and, certainly, the 18 chapters that follow this introduction cover an eye-stretching six decades.

These begin with his enlivening of a provincial upbringing with sexual adventure and tentative attempts to forge a more glamorous career than that suggested by his graduation from local state schools to the London School of Economics, and conclude with his present life as a knighted mainstay of rock's ruling class, an incorrigible but hugely successful *roué*; as poutingly athletic a showman as ever he was; one of the most astute and wealthiest wheeler-dealers in British business – and one who has gouged so deep a wound in pop that no poor-selling solo album, so-so movie, compromising elitism, affected mannerisms or any other past or future folly will allow the mere mortal that is Michael Philip Jagger to outlive the legend.

Neither can he ever be permitted to escape the orbit of The Rolling Stones, even if the group – and the consequent history of pop – would have been unthinkable without him. Raw fact boils down their formation as a rhythm-and-blues sextet in London around 1962. Their gimmick was long hair. The one who didn't have long hair wasn't allowed on stage with the other five. They had their first hit in 1963. They kept on having hits. Their singer had big lips and danced about. He became the most popular with the girls. The newspapers often printed stories about The Rolling Stones being rude. A big fuss was made when three of them went to prison for taking drugs but were let off. The one who took the most drugs then left and expired soon afterwards. All the same, the group continued to entertain people with much the same sort of music they'd always made.

Elaborations and regurgitations of the above information may be found in numerous internet websites and literary works dealing with both Jagger in particular and the Stones in general, from the broadest outline to the most meticulous detail – such as the third fingernail growing faster than the others on his left hand.[2] From their own ranks, there's been an autobiography by bass player Bill Wyman,[3] though one by Jagger himself foundered years ago. The most 'balanced' unauthorised view is that of Philip Norman,[4] but if it's salaciousness you're after, there's a tome by 'Spanish' Tony Sanchez – their narcotics dealer[5] – and, more recently, *Arise, Sir Mick: The True Story Of Britain's Naughtiest Knight* from a certain Laura Jackson.[6]

I know a Kentish landscape gardener whose Bible used to be the very first Stones memoir, *Our Own Story*, 'as we told it to Pete Goodman'.[7] His cousin had apparently 'been out' with Mick, but this relationship must have been purely platonic because, after a Boy Scout meeting in 1964, the patrol second of the Beavers assured me that Jagger was to undergo a sex-change operation so that he could marry one of the others. Two years later, another Scout, Kevin Delaney, spent nearly three hours pacing up and down outside a record shop, deliberating whether to blow three weeks' paper-round savings on *Aftermath*. At a wedding reception, his uncle, donning a woman's wig, had done a flawless imitation of 'that Mike Jaggers' as 'Satisfaction' shook the Dansette.

The accumulation of these incidents and disclosures added to my own adolescent confusion. In macho Baden-Powell circles, and brutalised by grammar school, it was still cool to like Stones *music*, but what couldn't be admitted was finding their androgyny guiltily transfixing. A simple image such as the cover of their debut EP – a pop Sarajevo assassination – could trigger a ten-year running battle with Authority over hair. With much the same attitude as a Great War trench private resigned to the stray bullet at Wipers, I would practise being Jagger before the bedroom mirror to the detriment of physics homework, and on the understanding that, within the hour, I could be eating my teenage heart out in front of that same mirror after an enforced visit to the barber.

It had, therefore, to be an imperceptible reverse-psychology process. Like *1984* and Winston Smith yelling public abuse at Goldstein, you'd tell your mother that the Stones were morons and join in the sniggers when Max Bygraves centred his jokes during one edition of ITV's *Sunday Night At The London Palladium* on a blow-up of Jagger with a Yul Brynner pate, while despising in secret comedians like Bygraves and Ted Rogers, who, knowing the prejudices of their audience, would only have to hold their noses and twang 'Ah wanna be your lover baby, ah wanna be your man' to get a laugh.

Long hair was a red rag to local cowboys as well as parents and teachers. In Aldershot Magistrates' Court in 1964, a hod-carrier accused of assaulting a complete stranger offered the plea, 'Well, he had long hair, hadn't he?' as a defence. Even when it became acceptable for studs to be hirsute, you could still get worked over out of jealousy by those whose coiffeur was governed by work conditions, such as members of the Armed Forces. Nevertheless, it made your day if some Oscar Wilde bawled 'Get yer 'air cut!' from a passing car while his grinning mates twisted around in the back seat to gauge the effect of this witticism on you. You weren't insulted. You were proud. At last you'd pulled wool over Authority's eyes long enough for it to show. By inviting persecution, you felt you were sharing something with the Stones.

Some went further than trying simply to look like a Stone. At 17, I rampaged through 'Sympathy For The Devil' to my own acoustic guitar accompaniment in church when the youth club was permitted by some with-it curate to take over Evensong one Sunday. Without the restraint of clutching an instrument, my interpretation of Jagger's stagecraft was among the factors that caused my underhanded but understandable dismissal from a folk-rock outfit named Turnpike in 1973.

Only in retrospect did I learn how wide of the mark my conception of the Stones' hard, flashy lifestyle was. In a conversation with former member Dick Taylor – now a friend of mine – I was half expecting him to be bitter and twisted about missing the millions. Instead, he was attractive in his phlegmatic candour, reflecting that if he'd stayed on, he, like Brian Jones, might have perished at an early age.

Of course, the Stones were always cheap. Fancy crediting chanting of hysterical girls as 'We Want The Stones', an opus 'composed' by Nanker-Phelge – the collective name given to items to which all personnel contributed. As if Sinatra would ever have covered that. Then there was the time they shared a Texas stage with performing seals. They were never above penny-pinching or even a good old-fashioned publicity stunt.

Yet it was their grubbing, arbitrary opportunism that brought them closer to home than the decorated Beatles. Lacking the studio freedom bequeathed by EMI, the Stones didn't so much compromise as deviously warp Decca's stringent traditions – as in their sly booking of off-peak hours in order to be unfettered by snoring studio managers. On other occasions, they threw in the towel, as in the matter of the *Beggars Banquet* graffiti sleeve. Such style wars were reflected in their fans' struggles against more parochial and domestic squares.

The Stones had detractors among their own rebel kind, too. In the late 1970s, many quarters of the music press waxed sycophantically about the glories of punk, damning the Stones with faint praise without acknowledging their precedents of outrage. A decade earlier, singing flautist Ian Anderson of Jethro Tull likewise bit the hand that fed him by slamming the Stones' musicianship, with pointed reference to Brian Jones.

Much of the criticism was well-founded, but essentially it didn't matter. Journalists have to make a living, even if it involves toadying to someone called Johnny Rotten. Who the hell are Jethro Tull, anyway? True, the Stones were as culpable as anyone else of bandwagon-jumping; witness the basic *Sgt Pepper* concept of the martyred *Satanic Majesties* and, specifically, Jagger's natural propensity to reinvent, even contradict, himself as the seasons of pop rotated.

This tendency surfaced time and time again during an exploration of what interested me – and what didn't – about both his personal circumstances and his place in the general scheme of things. In doing so, I tried to avoid the more familiar quotes and anecdotes. As well as often obscure press archives, this account has been drawn too from interviews with such as Rick Huxley (Jagger's cousin and member of The Dave Clark Five); Marsha Hunt, mother of his first child; Dick Taylor and other intimates who may prefer not to be mentioned.

I am grateful, too, for the reminiscences, clear insight and intelligent argument of Pat Andrews, Dave Berry, Don Craine, Keith Grant-Evans, Phil May, Jim McCarty, the late David Sanderson, Twinkle Rogers and Art Wood.

Please put your hands together for Chris Harvey, Albert DePetrillo, Tara O'Leary, Dicken Goodwin, Michael Wilson, Kathleen Meengs and Claire White at Sanctuary. I would also like to say a big 'hello!' to Iain MacGregor and Laura Brudenell.

Whether they were aware of providing assistance or not, let's also have a round of applause for these musicians: Frank Allen, Roger Barnes, Alan Barwise, Peter Barton, Arthur Brown, Mike Cooper, Pete Cox, Chris Dreja, Chris Gore, 'Wreckless' Eric Goulden, Brian Hinton, Alan Holmes, Robb Johnston, Garry

Jones, Graham Larkbey, Glen Matlock, Tom McGuiness, Andy Pegg, Brian Poole, Tom Robinson, Paul Samwell-Smith, Jim Simpson, Mike and Anja Stax, the late Lord David Sutch, John Townsend, Paul Tucker, Ron Watts and Fran Wood.

Thanks is also due in varying degrees to Stuart and Kathryn Booth, Tony Cousins, Robert Cross (of Bemish Business Machines), Kevin Delaney, Stefan Mlynek, Peter Doggett, Ian Drummond, Tim Fagan, Katy Foster-Moore, Gill Gore, Richard Hattrell, Michael Heatley, the late Susan Hill, Dave Humphreys, Rob Johnstone, Allan Jones, Mick and Sarah Jones, Elisabeth McCrae, Russell Newmark, Mike Ober, Mike Robinson, Mark and Stuart Stokes, Anna Taylor, Michael Towers, Warren Walters, Gina Way and Ted Woodings, as well as Inese, Jack and Harry Clayson.

Alan Clayson
October 2004

1 Go On To School

'It takes a conventional upbringing in the English style to produce a normal human being. It gives you an equilibrium, a balanced view.'

– Mick Jagger[1]

With the candour of encroaching old age, Mick Jagger made two separate and contrary assertions. The first was 'I always knew I'd be rich. I always thought I was special',[2] but a few years later he was 'just an ordinary English bloke, the same as everyone else'.[3]

His background wasn't untypical of an ordinary English bloke. As with most families, there was a real or invented affinity with someone vaguely famous. Apparently, an immediate ancestor, Joseph Hobson Jagger, inspired the music-hall song 'The Man Who Broke The Bank At Monte Carlo' by figuring out the secret of a principal casino's roulette wheel.

Looking forwards, Rick Huxley, Mick's cousin by marriage, was to be bass guitarist with The Dave Clark Five, a pop group that was to rack up hefty achievements in North America in a future unimaginable when two Rolling Stones – as well as two members of The Pretty Things – were all born during the Second World War at Livingstone Hospital in Dartford, one of north Kent's estuary towns, just outside the postal districts of Greater London.

Hitler's defeat was in distant sight when 30-year-old Basil Fanshawe Jagger – too young to have lost most of his hair – held his newborn son in the maternity ward on 26 July 1943, a dry, sunny and very warm Monday. Mr Jagger was known as 'Joe' to his loved ones, as the boy – christened Michael Philip – would be 'Mike' for most of the first two decades of his life.[4]

Joe had lived in Dartford only since 1938, and his accent and ideals would always betray more than a trace of a north-country Methodist upbringing: teetotal, God-fearing, modest to the point of invisibility, diligent at work, faithful in wedlock, provident of wise words and firm handling in parenthood, and nowhere near as open about sexual matters as his Nonconformist opposite number in the former slave states of the USA. 'My father is a Baptist minister,' explained Chuck Berry, a singing guitarist from St Louis, who'd loom large in the legend. 'He taught us, "Son, there's nothing wrong with sex. It's just the way you handle it."'[5]

Mr Jagger's courtship of Eva Scutts – a local hairdresser of exactly the same age, to the month – concluded with marriage in 1940. Eva was Australian by birth but educated in Dartford's Church of England state schools from age 4 to 16. Her husband was to teach physical education at one of them before an appointment as a lecturer in the same subject at a teacher-training college, where he was to collate accumulated knowledge about a sport that had just been introduced to Britain into a definitive book, *Basketball: Coaching And Playing.* His salary was ample enough to allow holidays abroad – a luxury then beyond the reach of most Britons – for a family that, shortly after Mike had started school, would embrace another child, Christopher, from Eva's second and final confinement, in December 1947.

Mrs Jagger was an orderly housewife, ensuring that the sugar was in its bowl, the milk in its jug, the cups unchipped on their saucers on an embroidered tablecloth. However, her self-ordained routine of spring cleaning had been disrupted earlier in 1947 by the build-up to the marriage of her brother-in-law to Rick Huxley's aunt. In a photograph snapped at the reception, two small boys are seated at arms-folded attention.

The translation of Rick and Mike to pop stardom was mostly a gradual development of unconscious forces rather than an oscillating series of lucky breaks, close shaves and chances in a million. Neither were from particularly musical families, 'even though the radio was usually humming with Victor Sylvester or Edmundo Ros', as Jagger later recalled. 'Our mother sang and danced around, and her brothers were on the fringe of music hall. Hymn-singing was big with the Methodists, and our nan used to belt out a tune at parties.'[6]

Of the Jagger siblings, Chris seemed to have the most natural aptitude, piping out light-opera arias in an uncertain treble in his bedroom and an unaccompanied 'The Deadwood Stage (Whip-Crack-Away)' – from the 1953 film *Calamity Jane* – during an end-of-term concert at Maypole Infants' School, where Mike had preceded him as a pupil. The older boy's interest in music stemmed from listening to military bands trumping marches at Remembrance Day parades, all the more proudly dignified since 1945.

One consequence of victory in the Second World War was that the quayside garrisons and naval depots in nearby Chatham ceased to spoonfeed bloodshed in the English Channel and North Sea. Another was the carving of a huge cross where a Spitfire had been shot down in the chalky turf on a hill that could be seen from the windows of cars *en route* to Maidstone, Kent's county town. On the way back to Dartford, you'd read *Tenez la gauche* and *Links Fahren* on roadsigns reminding foreign drivers off the ferry from Dover to drive on the left as they flitted between the post-war conurbations that had been swallowing up areas of the so-called 'Garden of England' since the Industrial Revolution.

Communities that escaped being thus absorbed had endured too many hard winters to harbour any illusions that they dwelt in a rural arcadia. Hop-picking might have been a working holiday for some, but it was just plain working for others. In certain far-flung hamlets, tap water was still a council election promise, while in the poorer urban districts, gas rather than electricity lit kitchens where margarine was spread instead of butter and noisy copper geysers hung above sinks in which a mother would both bathe babies and wash dishes from a Sunday lunch on a newspaper tablecloth.

Yet, with her sense of hearing not yet dulled by the ever-increasing volume of traffic, it was easy to differentiate between individual sounds of local vehicles belonging to, say, the district nurse, the vicar, the publican – or the milkman, if his crates weren't being transported by a plodding pony instead.

Even in households like the Jaggers' in upmarket Wilmington – a village-like suburb of Dartford – wireless sets were novel enough to be regarded by censorious great-aunts as meddling with dark forces. Just suppose you were 'taken' when listening to that repulsive Johnnie Ray's smutty 'Such A Night' on the BBC Light Programme. You'd be cast into the everlasting pit like the Whore of Babylon. Think on that!

Anticipating the narcissistic exhibitionism that would pervade rock 'n' roll, Johnnie Ray – a jazz-influenced entertainer from the USA – was the wildest act going in an age when pop was seen (in Britain, anyway) as a preliminary for a life as an 'all-round entertainer'. After notching up a handful of hits, a singer would 'mature' – and a sure sign that he or she had thus Made It was a prime-time duet on black-and-white television of an old evergreen with someone like Royal Command Performance veteran Max Bygraves, prefaced by scripted ad-libbing between cheeky young shaver and jovial voice-of-experience.

Funnymen like Bygraves, Dave King and Bob Monkhouse were more likely focuses of adoration than pop singers at that time. Ted Lune – idiotic 'Private Bone' in *The Army Game*, a sitcom on the new ITV television channel – passed through cheering streets when he returned in on-screen costume to his home town of Blackburn. Parrot-like in profile, bug-eyed, skinny and Jodrell Bank-eared, Lune was a celebrity you didn't mind your girlfriend liking. More of a threat were the 'sensible' likes of Eamonn Andrews, David Attenborough, sports commentator Peter West, crooner Dickie Valentine, newsreader Huw Wheldon and others omnipresent on British television when Mike Jagger graduated from Wentworth Juniors to Dartford Grammar School in 1954.

If no gangling Ted Lune type, Mike didn't look like he'd match up, either, to the handsome, clean-cut manliness of Andrews, Attenborough *et al*. Just under middle height, with a slender frame and auburn-to-mousy hair kept to regulation short back and sides, his most distinguishing feature was inherited from his mother: wide, loose and over-generous lips that, in repose, drooped to an expression construed as 'insolent' by masters at the Grammar, where he would be in the top arts stream by the third year.

Genuine surliness contorted his face through a dislike of the uniform (especially the cap) and physical exercise, 'but I know I have to do it'.[7] Yet, despite seeming to despise an inbred ability, he shone at cricket, rugby and badminton, was a luminary of the basketball team, and at 18, was to obtain a holiday job as a PE instructor at a US air base just beyond Dartford. Moreover, four years earlier, Mike made a mute television debut in the ITV children's magazine *Seeing Sport*, along with Joe (also its technical advisor), for an edition broadcast from Tunbridge Wells. The show depicted them scaling a rock face and erecting a tent, but the clip to be most commonly used in those before-they-were-famous TV compilations that rear up periodically nowadays, would be the presenter pointing out the practicality of Mike's hard-wearing plimsolls.

To classmates, he spoke no more about *Seeing Sport* than he would about being obliged to go to church. Indeed, he proclaimed himself an atheist and, in the 'common' sub-Cockney drawl he assumed outside Wilmington, spoke confidentially about sex as if he had inside information about it. They didn't want to believe he did, but Dick Taylor, a builder's son from Bexleyheath, observed that his friend 'always seemed to have multiple girlfriends, and was very active in that department before the rest of us. He was forever in the coffee bar in Dartford, chatting up some girl.'

This overriding interest would metamorphose into a constant and relentless search for variety, even provoking spurious whispers in the all-boys school of homosexual experimentation. His main targets, however, were females more dauntingly free-spirited than the usual *nice* girl of the mid-1950s, 'saving herself' for her wedding night. A nurse at Bexley Mental Hospital was reputed to have been the first to – ahem – surrender herself fully to Mike's picaresque charm when he was working there as a porter during a summer recess.

Equally precocious was Jagger's appreciation that, with the arrival of rock 'n' roll from North America, pop's erotic content was no longer as cloaked in stardust and roses. Culturally window-shopping, he spared surprisingly little time for Elvis Presley's embroidered shout-singing and sulky balladeering, much preferring the more unhinged go-man-go sorcery of Little Richard, whose effeminate manner had led his very father to disown him. In billowing drapes and precarious pompadour, Richard's bombastic vocal delivery swooped from roar to shriek in 'Rip It Up', 'Long Tall Sally' and, climactically, 'Tutti Frutti' – sexual doggerel sanitised to joyous gibberish and, therefore, palatable to a white public – while he punished a grand piano with parts of his anatomy apart from his fingers in *Don't Knock The Rock*, a movie of thin plot that reached Dartford in 1957.

Mike Jagger wondered from whence such glorious row was traceable. Perhaps not yet aware that the likes of Little Richard, Fats Domino and Chuck Berry were black, he assumed initially that it was derived from the 'hard' country and western of Hank Williams, Merle Haggard and Johnny Cash, as opposed to Jim Reeves/Slim Whitman 'sweetcorn'. He later discovered that this was indeed the case, in the sense that Williams, Haggard and Cash borrowed from blues just as Berry, Domino and – to a smaller degree – Richard did from C&W.

If there was a specific road-to-Damascus moment for Mike, it was – according to another school chum, Peter Holland – when one of the catering staff at the US encampment introduced him to the blues one afternoon around a record player. Something enormous took place. Yet, though instantly transfixed, the young man had no idea how to set about obtaining the records until he learned from Dick Taylor – already a collector – of the existence of Dobell's in central London and Carey's Swing Shop in Streatham, stores that specialised in a wide spectrum of imported merchandise from black America, whether the rural stumblings of Snooks Eaglin, Robert Johnson or Champion Jack Dupree; Chicago and New Orleans rhythm and blues – R&B – via the likes of Domino, Smiley Lewis, Muddy Waters, Howlin' Wolf and (of particular appeal to Jagger) Jimmy Reed; or towards the badlands of rock 'n' roll via Chuck Berry and Bo Diddley.

Mike and Dick were to lend an intrigued rather than obsessed ear to Buddy Holly, a bespectacled white Texan who 'was sort of halfway', noted Dick. 'His brand of rock 'n' roll was half country, half blues.' With members of his backing Crickets, Holly composed simple but atmospheric songs tailored to his elastic adenoids. 'We both thought that "Not Fade Away" was the best thing Buddy ever did,' enthused Taylor, 'though it was only a B-side.'

Part of the attraction was a demonstration that rock 'n' roll could be simultaneously forceful and romantic, and that it could progress without getting too complex. While 'Not Fade Away' hinged on the trademark 'shave and a haircut, six pence' rhythm by this Bo Diddley fellow, another B-side, 'I'm Looking For Someone To Love', hinged on standard blues chord changes. Neither did Buddy and the Crickets make fools of themselves when tackling black non-originals. More intense than gut-wrenching, if Holly broke sweat on, say, Little Richard's 'Slippin' And Slidin'', sonorous wordless harmonies from his colleagues kept him cool so that the song could surge to a climax all the more rewarding for the restraint that preceded it.

Like Jagger and Taylor, Ahmet and Nesuhi Ertegun, sons of a Turkish diplomat based in the USA, were listeners rather than performers. They were so in love with pop that bordered on blues – and jazz – that Ahmet formed his very own record company, Atlantic, and Nesuhi promoted concerts. In 1955, Ahmet brought

his older brother into Atlantic to develop the jazz side of the label while he himself concentrated on blues and R&B. In Chicago, a victim of the same passion, an Americanised Pole named Leonard Chess, founded Chess Records for the same purpose.

Of course, neither Chess nor the Erteguns could have understood to what extent their lives would interweave with that of an English schoolboy whose closest encounter with in-person US pop was when he, Dick Taylor and two other Dartford Grammar pals – Alan Etherington and Robert Beckwith – saw Buddy Holly in March 1958 during his only British tour. This was perhaps the most pivotal of all the events that coalesced to produce the British beat boom, for among other lads who found Holly and his musicians' stage act and compact sound instructive were Dave Clark, Brian Poole, Jeff Beck, Keith Relf and Eric Clapton, who, independently of each other, all caught the show in and around London, too. Not lost to Mike Jagger, either, was that Holly was more Ted Lune than Elvis Presley, and yet girls still screamed at him.

After he played the Liverpool Empire, John Lennon and Paul McCartney's early efforts as songwriters became less of a sideline. At the Manchester stop were future Hollies Allan Clarke and Graham Nash and a spindly youth named Garrity, lately parted from a girlfriend who'd disapproved of him singing in a new group called Freddie And The Dreamers, in which he wore Holly-like spectacles – as would Brian Poole after he'd approached lads at his Barking secondary school about forming his own Crickets with himself as Buddy.

After Buddy Holly returned to the States, it was no coincidence that sales of electric guitars boomed, especially those of either genuine or copied sunburst Fenders the same as his. Mike Jagger, however, made do with an acoustic six-string purchased when the family spent a week in Spain. He used a pyjama cord as a strap so that it could hang from his shoulders when he posed in front of a bedroom mirror and put one of his growing pile of records on the turntable, curling his lip, shaking his hips and mouthing the lyrics, yeah-ing and uh-huh-ing.

Dick Taylor and Rick Huxley had each taken the trouble to learn properly, even as they revised for the General Certificate of Education O-level examinations that would enable Dick to enrol at an art college in Sidcup and Rick at Gravesend Technical College. With an impressive seven O-level passes, Mike Jagger chose to join the academic elite in Dartford Grammar's sixth form.

Before the Huxleys moved to Kentish Town in north London in 1958, Mike and Rick would sometimes try in vain to sit in with outfits that played at the Railway Hotel – a Dartford pub with a music licence – but they imagined that they'd grow out of rock 'n' roll, cast it aside as an adolescent folly. Besides, it wasn't how good you were; it was who you knew in the business, wasn't it? Mike didn't know anyone apart from some chaps in a couple of groups at school.

One night, in readiness for a dance organised jointly with the sixth form at a sister establishment, one such outfit, The Southerners, were setting up puny amplifiers to power Buddy Holly guitars and warming up voices yet to spit out home-counties plums. From the dusty half-light beyond footlights still being tested, Mike Jagger stepped to the foot of the stage to ask meekly if he could sing with them that evening.

Politely rebuffed, he bore no grudge, and next approached Danny Rogers And His Realms. Their guitarist, Alan Dow – now a structural engineer, and looking very pleased with himself in the present-day photograph alongside an article about his pop past in Reading's *Evening Post* – remembered 'Mike Jagger coming up to me during an interval in a sixth form concert. He asked, "Can I do a few numbers with you?" I said, "No, Mike. I think we are all right." He was playing all these weird records that no-one else wanted to listen to.'[8]

2 Boogie In The Dark

'Jagger, Pete Townshend, McCartney, Lennon were all intellectual appreciators of this foreign form. The Brits took it much more seriously.'

– Ahmet Ertegun[1]

These 'weird records' of which Mike Jagger was inordinately fond were of a genre that he hadn't been able to touch at first. His function, then, was just to absorb the signals as they came. Blues was peculiar to black American experience[2] and usually purchasable only after having wended their way across the ocean to outlets like Dobell's and Carey's Swing Shop.

Mike was also receiving mailed lists and order forms from untold US independent labels like Excello, Aladdin, Atlantic and Imperial, and had been writing directly to Leonard Chess. Even when British labels began issuing R&B singles such as James Brown's 'Think' (on Parlophone in 1961) and material in all vinyl formats by Bo Diddley, Howlin' Wolf, Muddy Waters and other executants of the sacred sounds (via Pye International's R&B series), letters arrived from Jagger in Wilmington entreating the companies to issue more.

In Britain, blues in each of its subdivisions remained, to all intents and purposes, the exclusive property of a knotted-brow fringe. It was a comparatively unknown quantity even in the USA, hovering in mainstream pop as distant thunder, at most. Indeed, releases by such as Jimmy Reed, Muddy Waters and Howlin' Wolf sold by the ton in Uncle Sam's 'race' or 'sepia' market without figuring at all in music-trade periodical *Billboard*'s Hot 100 pop chart. Yet blues wasn't particularly popular amongst citified young blacks, being music that their migrant parents still liked.

Back in the rural Deep South, Buddy Knox, a rock 'n' roller from the same region as Buddy Holly, couldn't recall hearing a single disc by a black singer until he visited New York – although, through radio static, others his age might have tuned in by accident to muffled bursts of what white segregationists heard as 'the screaming idiotic words and savage music' of faraway Streveport's rhythm-and-blues station KWKH, where 'Stan The Man And His No-Name Record Jive' spun The Midnighters' 'Sexy Ways', 'Sixty-Minute Man' by The Dominoes and 'Too Many Drivers' by Smiley Lewis – all about sex and all banned from white radio. 'If you don't want to serve negroes in your place of business,' ran one racist handbill, 'then do not have negro records on your juke-box.'

For Britons insensible of ingrained racial tension, such discs – when they got around to hearing them – were 'something new and exciting', deduced Ahmet Ertegun. 'In a sense, they were appreciating something the Americans did not value.'[1]

Taking up the theme, Jagger continued, 'As far as white people were concerned – especially suburban kids – it was interesting because it was underclass music that they'd had no experience of, or, in fact, that didn't exist by the time they had got to it anyway, almost. It was disappearing. That culture was on its way out.'[3]

Because Dartford Grammar was slightly less shrouded in the draconian affectations and futile rigmarole prevalent in other schools, it wasn't completely malevolent towards, for instance, Jagger alluding to 'the strange and cruel origins of the blues'[4] and 'blues- and jazz-influenced pop singers', and using Bo Diddley as a case study – with audio-visual aids – when delivering a talk to the history society about his now-overwhelming passion.

Quoting Jimmy Reed titles[5] and lyrics as if they were proverbs, and in the thick of every common-room controversy to do with the music of black America, Mike also entered into occasional debate on the letters page of *Record Mirror*, ready at any moment with a corrective tirade against other correspondents. Neither did he hesitate to attack the paper's very journalists. He was certainly more knowledgeable about the subject than most of them.

Being mad about the blues might have been a more socially acceptable pastime than, say, accumulating information about donkeys' false teeth or annotating the reference matrixes of electricity pylons, but with a madcap obsession beyond mere enthusiasm a Newcastle art student named Eric Burdon had ritually inked the word 'BLUES' in his own blood across the cover of an exercise book in which lyrics of the same had been compiled.

Though Burdon was embroiled in the formation of a group of like-minded musicians, Manchester's Bodega Jazz Club had hosted the debut of an outfit led by 17-year-old boogie-woogie pianist John Mayall as early as 1950, and blues had also infiltrated the repertoire of a foremost London jazz band led by trombonist Chris Barber, chiefly through its contingent skiffle-playing Washboard Wonders trio, fronted by the celebrated Lonnie Donegan. In 1960's sniffy *A Guide To Popular Music*, written by staff at Decca – one of the country's four major record companies at the time – this 'skiffle' music was defined as 'a makeshift kind of jazz, played on standard instruments mixed with the home-made'.[6]

In a school essay on skiffle, Mike Jagger contended that, 'before any group is started up, there should be someone who can sing really well, and a couple of guitarists who can play good, strong chords'.[7] This was received wisdom from Lonnie Donegan, who, after leaving the Barber band, had bossed the ensuing craze in Britain throughout its 1957 prime and beyond. Though he was to offend purists by tilting for wider acceptance with such as the Boy Scouts' campfire ditty 'Does Your Chewing Gum Lose Its Flavour' and 1960's chart-topping 'My Old Man's A Dustman', Lonnie's impact would ripple across aeons of British pop through his impregnating an impoverished and imitative scene with energetic alien idioms and a mesmeric whine far removed from the docile plumminess of other native pop vocalists.

Skiffle's closest US equivalent was rockabilly, a strand of rock 'n' roll based likewise on sparse instrumentation and primeval rowdiness. Anyone with a little imagination who'd mastered basic techniques could give skiffle a try, with artists such as Cliff Richard, The Beatles, Van Morrison, The Troggs, Alex Harvey and Gary Glitter amongst examples from subsequent pop generations who did just that.

Belatedly, so too did Mike Jagger and Dick Taylor, with the discovery that their unorthodox musical vision was shared with other renegades disenchanted with the assembly-line pop in which the likes of The Southerners and Danny Rogers traded. Listening sessions had evolved into endeavours at replicating the unpopular sounds themselves. Guitars were picked by Taylor, Robert Beckwith and Alan Etherington, with Alan and Dick doubling respectively on maracas and the latter's grandfather's 'tiny, ancient drum kit'. Robert was the first of the group to screw an electronic pickup over the hole in his instrument. When the others followed his lead, the guitars were fed through tape recorders and Dick's older sister's record-player – as was a microphone through which Mike sang and blew a mouth organ, neither of which imposed restriction on movement. 'My mum was fascinated by him,' smiled Taylor, 'loved his singing and dancing around. He was leaping about like a lunatic.'

During pauses during which he lubricated his throat with *Bing* – a fizzy drink peculiar to Kent – there was little discussion about the quality of Mike's vocals. From the beginning, it was close enough in timbre and pitch to some of the black icons he admired that the others took it for granted. Consciously trying to imitate, say, laconic Slim Harpo, bestial Howlin' Wolf or unruffled Chuck Berry, his still-breaking voice was corrupted for all time with a piquancy devoid of vowel purity and nicety of intonation. Instead, you got slovenly diction, disjointed range and a vehemence dredged up from the constrictions of his neck rather than the flexibility of the diaphragm, a technique that would render it beyond the pale by European *bel canto* standards.

His mother didn't like it much, and said so whenever the fellows practised upstairs. If she put her head around the door, the music – which had a ragged dissimilarity to any pop she'd ever heard – would shudder to a halt. Most rehearsals took place thereafter at the Taylors' or the Etheringtons'. To what purpose was never clear; none of the members could even speak their group's name – Little Boy Blue And The Blue Boys – without affectation. Neither did anyone attempt to procure a public engagement nor consider an opinion held by Bob Cort – one of skiffle's lesser icons – concerning visual effect: 'Some sort of uniform is a great help, though casual clothes are perhaps the best, as long as you look exactly the same.'[8]

As skiffle latecomers, however, they agreed with Cort's pontification that 'That's where half the enjoyment lies – in experimenting with ideas.'[8] Though they'd educated themselves in their preferred aspect of the music that lay beneath and fluttered above the form's chewing-gum-flavoured veneer, Little Boy Blue And The Blue Boys made one irresistible concession to mainstream pop in 'La Bamba' by Ritchie Valens, remembered chiefly as one who'd been killed in the same aeroplane crash as Buddy Holly. Otherwise, it was blues – of urban rather than rural persuasion – and almost nothing but. There was a lot from Jimmy Reed's and Bo Diddley's portfolios, and nods to Wolf and Waters, but statistically Chuck Berry won, hands down.

Berry was also the US rhythm-and-blues exponent that most awed fans on the opposite coast of the Straits of Dover – where Paris was nearer to Dartford than Newcastle or Plymouth – for his neo-Gallic equality of words and tune. Indeed, one of France's first homogenous stabs at rock 'n' roll was Les Chaussettes Noires' 'Johnny B Goode' (as 'Eddie Sois Bon'), Berry's signature tune. Yet, although the spirit was willing, pop stars *sur le continent* tended to be raucous, not passionate, if they got as far as shedding enough of their inhibitions to cut up rough. *Dans leurs peaux* about a second-class status, they were glad to breathe the air around such as Gene Vincent – so renowned in France that he'd find himself there time and time again over years of dogged touring – and Vince Taylor, a vocalist from Middlesex, who virtually took up French citizenship.

The biggest stumbling block was that rock 'n' roll had developed into an English-language music, and would remain so for all time. Even on static-ridden radio, reproductions of Chuck Berry sounded nowhere near as accurate as they did on our side of the Channel, where 'Carol', 'Reelin' And Rockin'', 'You Can't Catch Me', 'Little Queenie' and all the rest of them were to be prominent in the repertoires of all British beat groups that counted, and were often the redeeming features of many that didn't.

By 1960, however, Chuck was in jail, Buddy Holly was dead and Little Richard had taken holy orders. Dickie Valentine – now a 30-year-old father of two – had just released the ill-advised 'Teenager In Love', and Max Bygraves had seen in the new decade with the expedient and jogalong 'Jingle Bell Rock', climbing to Number Seven in the hit parade, while on its way to Number Two was borderline-religious 'A Voice In The Wilderness' by Cliff Richard, who'd been elevated from provincial skiffler to the status of 'English Elvis' and was in the process of following the real Presley's new path as all-round family entertainer. It was difficult for Mike Jagger to comprehend why one so tamed had once appalled his own mother, who 'would watch my lovely boys, sitting so neat and clean, watching that dreadful Cliff Richard, that awful hair and that sexy dancing'.[9]

By then, 'skiffle' had become a vile word for Mike and other hip sixth formers, now that a Camberwell curate's *Skiffle Mass* – making a cheerful noise unto the God of Jacob – had been among abominations seized upon as a means of nurturing youthful Christianity. Barren booking schedules forced many a still-functioning skiffle ensemble back to church-organised young people's clubs, where part of the deal might be that their set was to be interrupted by a 'spontaneous' on-mic dialogue between the vicar – exclaiming 'too much', 'squaresville' and other transatlantic expressions he imagined teenagers still used – and one of his juvenile flock. They'd chat about sin. His Reverence would be against it.

That such a booking was a necessary evil for a provincial combo short of bookings, it was small wonder that Little Boy Blue And The Blue Boys had turned into less a group than a musical-appreciation society when Mike Jagger's GCE A-level results alighted onto his doormat. Even prior to passing two – history and English literature – vocational stock-taking had had him applying for a course focused principally on economics and political science at the London School of Economics, within walking distance of both the bustling consumers' paradises centred on Oxford Street and the back alleys that spread from Soho Square, proliferating with striptease joints, illicit gambling dens and clandestine brothels. Jagger might have been an arts student, but, as his A-level grades weren't brilliant, 'Lofty' Hudson – Dartford Grammar's headmaster – in his office as careers advisor, laid on the LSE with a trowel. Mike did not know then that, over the years, Lofty had worked up some influence with the interviewing panel.

If modelled on L'École Libre des Sciences Politiques in Paris, the LSE was a British university by any other name. Nevertheless, while it wasn't yet the New Left hotbed it would become, Leninists looked down on Trotskyists there and words like *bourgeoisie*, *existentialist* and *materialism* buzzed around the corridors. Other than lecturers and mature students, everyone occupied that awkward stage where they were deciding where and where not to grow up. Most obviously, clothes polarised each social group. Grey flannel trousers, twinsets and chunky hair glaciated with spray or brilliantine stated that either you hadn't yet escaped the clutches of parents who expected you to be a credit to them, or that you accepted with hardly a murmur the promise of jam tomorrow if you beavered away, kept your nose clean and gained your degree.

On the other side of the sartorial coin were beatnik girls wearing either no makeup at all or a detergent-white mask relieved by black eyeshade and lipstick, conducting themselves as if in a trance and hiding their figures inside baggy jumpers annexed from existentialist boyfriends who either contrived to keep a day away from a shave or went a bit more of the whole hog with bumfluff beards like half-plucked versions of Fidel Castro's. Their manner of dressing implied falsely that they were unaware of the clothes they had flung on after rising that day.

Mike Jagger walked an uncomfortable line between the two extremes. If anything, he could be classed as a 'Millet' in his nylon pullover and yet-unfaded jeans from the Dartford branch of the store of the same name selling outdoor clothing and camping equipment. Draped round his neck was the LSE's official broad, striped scarf. Gilding the indeterminate image was that, to his father's dismay, he had started smoking.

His first cigarette of the day was usually when waiting among the bowler hats and furled umbrellas for the commuter train at Dartford railway station. Lighting up and inhaling casually but deeply, he was trying to impress girls who might have been making circuitous enquiries about him, as he'd been about them. Him and his sort were about to be caricatured in a spin-off 45 from the stars of *Eggheads*, a transient BBC television series of 1961 starring Bryan Blackburn and Peter Reeves – a sort of Newman and Baddiel of their day – portraying Jagger and his ilk as being on a constant quest for female favours on the premise that 'if she thinks you're kind of brainy, she flips'.[10]

Yet, while the daily journey to and from Holborn via British Rail and the London Underground system was still a novelty, Mike wasn't regarding it and his subsequent hours at the LSE entirely as a forum for initiating carnal adventures. Indeed, he seemed to be applying himself to his studies as if he almost meant to become a middle-weight financial executive in five years' time, on the board of directors in ten and chairman by the time he was 40.

It was to have a lasting and beneficial effect. Walter Yetnikoff, a record-company executive with whom Jagger had dealings as a world-famous Rolling Stone, would perceive later that 'his image as the prancing prince of rock belied the side of his character that had seriously studied economics. When it came to numbers, Mick was as sober as St Augustine.'[10] During one business lunch, he and Yetnikoff calculated on cocktail napkins a specific territory's VAT for a given royalty rate and number of albums sold. 'Two minutes later, he had an accurate reading,' goggled Yetnikoff, 'while I was still fumbling.'[11]

3 Outskirts Of Town

'Nobody wanted what we wanted to play because they
couldn't understand anyone wanting to hear it.'

– Mick Jagger[1]

Little Boy Blue And The Blue Boys survived its various members'
transfers from Dartford Grammar to higher education. Indeed,
the group now had a new guitarist, a pal of Dick's from Sidcup
Art College who didn't only like Chuck Berry; he worshipped him.
No other verb will do. Keith Richards worshipped Chuck Berry.

Richards had also been in Mike's year at Wentworth Primary,
but he had never been more than a common acquaintance. Paths
diverged when Keith's family moved to an overspill estate on the
wrong side of Dartford. Jagger next became aware of Richards
as a rather rat faced and under-nourished boy with a slouch and
garb that indicated direct descent from the Teddy Boys, narcissistic
tearaways who'd been the most menacing British youth cult of
the 1950s.

One of Mike's holiday jobs had involved selling ice creams
outside the public library. Keith remembered buying one when,
thrown together one morning in a smoking compartment of the
train to Sidcup and then London, he and Mike had granted each
other an irresolute nod and exchanged desultory platitudes. Under
normal circumstances, Keith might have then lost himself in his
thoughts, gazing at without seeing the over-familiar shopping
precincts, recreation grounds and waste-piped backs of buildings
hurtling by. Yet he was roused from his customary lethargy, not

by babble penetrating from outside at the next station, but on spying the front of one of the LPs Mike had about his person. It was Chuck Berry's *Rockin' At The Hop*, unissued in Britain and a priceless rarity to Keith.

He spoke aloud, forgetting both the other passengers and a natural shyness. It was as if he was watching himself in a play. With a hand on each knee and beaming from ear to ear, Keith met Mike's eyes through the nicotine haze, and demanded to know how he'd acquired such a precious object. There followed a cordial discussion that might have led nowhere had not Dick Taylor's name cropped up. When Mike waved from the window at Sidcup and went back to his peace, it had been agreed that Keith was to attend the next Blue Boys session.

It had been on another journey along the same route that Rick Huxley, returning from a visit to Dartford, had seen a scuffed page of *Melody Maker* on the carriage floor and had checked out the 'Musicians Wanted' column and Dave Clark's advertisement for like-minded players to join what would be his Five. Rick had already passed through the ranks of Kentish Town's Riverside Blues Boys, less specialist than his cousin's outfit and sporting a stage costume of blue suits with white ties.[2] Next, Huxley had been one of The Spon Valley Stompers, walking a line between blues and trad(itional) jazz, a pop phenomenon that, like skiffle, was peculiar to Britain alone.

A line in the 'Eggheads' single had namechecked 'Freud, Proust – and Acker Bilk', and to the man in the street, trad was epitomised by this bowler-hatted Somerset clarinettist. It had undergone such a revival around 1961 that Bilk and several other of its practitioners had made the charts. Then the trad network spread from parish halls and pub back rooms to venues that had once been the exclusive domain of skifflers who had backslid via amplification to rock 'n' roll and a UK Top 20 dominated by North Americans.

If big-time aspirations entered the equation, Little Boy Blue And The Blue Boys were therefore doomed unless they pulled some stroke that would lift them beyond just mucking about around each other's houses. Without pushing or showing off, Keith Richards was playing an increasingly more lively part in their still-covert activities as a close friendship with Mike took hold. Without purposely snubbing anyone, the two were seeking each other's particular company and evolving a restricted code that few outsiders could crack, not even Dick Taylor. The personal dynamic and interaction between them would intensify to such a degree that Jagger would later chortle, 'He was born my brother by accident, by different parents!'[1]

Mrs Jagger's disapproval of Keith's loutish demeanour and appearance was a point in his favour, as far as Mike was concerned, now that the emotional pressure 'to be good', to be worthy of all Eva and Joe had given to him and Chris, was beginning to take its toll, just when they'd imagined that Mike was over the developmental stage known as 'rebellious adolescence' (expressed most conspicuously in his inverted snobbery) and was changing – not via a lightning conversion, it was true, but slowly – into a serious, thoughtful young adult, applying himself industriously to his degree course.

It was worrying to witness contents merging between Mike and his dubious new best friend. They started to copy each other's idiosyncrasies, to dress and sculpt their hair similarly, Mike exchanging 'sensible shoes' for winkle-pickers and drainpiping his jeans so tightly that it looked as if his legs had been dipped in ink. As a final act of class betrayal, he was now styling himself 'Mick', as if he was the son of some London-Irish navvy.

While the differences between 'Mick' and Keith had consolidated their friendship, so equally did all that they had in common, most obviously a musical taste that stretched the envelope of blues to encompass Chuck Berry, Bo Diddley and even The Coasters, a black vocal group on the Atlantic label with a 'fool' bass singer and gimmick records like 'Yakety Yak' and 'Charlie Brown'.

Not everyone in Little Boy Blue And The Blue Boys was of like mind, however. Nevertheless, there remained sufficient sense of oneness for Mick, Keith, Dick and the other two to voyage far west to where blues had hit the metropolitan suburb of Ealing. Two former Chris Barber sidemen, mouth-organist Cyril Davies and guitarist Alexis Korner, were presiding over Blues Incorporated – not so much an R&B group as an R&B revivalist group – in their newly opened G Club, on Ealing's main thoroughfare.

It wasn't exactly the flower of England's young manhood setting off for Flanders, but from Middlesex, Surrey and other southern shires they came – along with fanatics like Eric Burdon, who'd hitchhiked all the way from Newcastle – to merge into the shadows of the basement sweatbath where Blues Incorporated held sway. It wasn't somewhere you went to chase girls until they caught you, not just because most of the patrons were male but also because of a pervading solemnity whereby the temptations of the flesh deferred to grim, knowing enjoyment of instrumental prowess and, paradoxically, songs about lust, violence and social disease, bereft of Top 20 euphemisms about dream lovers and teen angels. 'It was a Mecca for anyone interested in the blues,' confirmed Mick Jagger. 'We went every Saturday.'[3]

From the outset, it was clear to Mick that there was no artistic force-field surrounding Blues Incorporated like there'd been around The Southerners and Danny Rogers And His Realms. In theory, while it helped if you had a connection to the inner circle, anyone – the hopeful, the hopeless and the just plain starstruck – could step up from the audience and join Alexis, Cyril *et al* on the bandstand. Some would be waved in just because they happened to be holding a guitar, because they'd mentioned that they sang a bit or simply because Korner or Davies liked some facet of their personality.

One Sunday night, Cyril had caught The Art Wood Combo at the Blue Circle, in Ruislip. Its leader was promptly recruited to the ranks of Blues Incorporated, following a tutorial by Alexis. 'He came round my house with the words of a Muddy Waters number,' recollected Art Wood, 'asking if I could learn them in time for the following night. He sort of tutored me through it, to make me do it dirty enough, nasty enough. Before that, I was singing it too sweetly. He made me put more feeling into it by emphasising certain words.'

More prominent, physically, than Wood was a second singer, the imposing Long John Baldry, whose clean-shaven, light complexion beneath a neat blond crop made you think of Hitler's Aryan exemplar. Art was dwarfed too by Paul Jones, down from Oxford, where he'd been in a blues outfit with Brian Jones, an unrelated all-round musician who distinguished himself at the G Club with a stunning display of bottleneck-style electric guitar. Later on, the microphone would be lowered for a 15-year-old Cockney named Steve Marriott, in the midst of his 18 months of 'Food, Glorious Food' as The Artful Dodger in the West End musical *Oliver!* and recording two flop Buddy Holly-ish singles for Decca. Yet Marriott put up a surprisingly good show as a black soul in a white skin.

The North American genuine article would be represented by two black US servicemen awaiting imminent demobilisation. Urged by both Korner and customer reaction, Ronnie Jones and Herbie Goins decided to seek their fortunes as entertainers in Britain, Herbie forming a backing unit named The Night Timers for himself with Ronnie, who was very much the junior partner, taking on material thought unsuitable for Goins.

From Blues Incorporated too would spring The Rolling Stones, for reasons to do with the Korner outfit's intrinsic adulteration of R&B, despite the enlistment of Goins and his sidekick. 'Blues Incorporated was more of a jazz band,' explained Mick. 'Alexis sang these funny blues interpretations in what seemed to us a very upper-class English accent. We used to hoot with laughter about this. I saw people my own age getting up, and I thought to myself, "They're not that brilliant," so I got up and sang. Before I knew it, I was one of the band's featured vocalists. Then Keith would come up and we'd do a couple of Chuck Berry things. That's how it started.'[3]

'It' was prefaced by a tape – of Valens's 'La Bamba', Jimmy Reed's 'Bright Lights, Big City' *magnum opus* and two Berry items – mailed from Dick Taylor's address to an unimpressed Korner, who returned it.[4] Even so, Alexis raised no objections when, the following Saturday, Mick volunteered to play one of its selections, 'Around And Around', backed by Dick, Keith and anyone in the house band who wanted to play along.

Mick stubbed out a cigarette, cleared his throat and stood before the microphone, motionless bar trembling knees. The hubbub subdued to frozen faces staring up at him. He nearly felt sick, but a deep breath later he was into the opening line: 'Well, the joint was rockin'…' Glistening with embarrassment as the number died away, Mick's head fell before he glanced up with an enquiring eyebrow. A spatter of clapping for his nerve as much as his singing ensued. So began Mick Jagger's flight to the very pinnacle of pop, a fact not much appreciated on the night, least of all by Mick himself as he helped Keith and Dick heave their guitars and amplifiers onto the late train back to Kent.

There'd been a little self-conscious head-shaking – as if trying to slough off the onlookers' hushed attention – but, with and without Richards and Taylor for musical and moral support, Jagger slipped into a higher gear during subsequent G Club performances, such as a duet of Reed's 'I Ain't Got You' with Eric Burdon, quite tickled when anyone cried encouragement to him. He even hazarded blowing harmonica in the teeth of Cyril Davies's grouchy 'Get a pair of pliers' when he sought advice on how to bend notes.

Mick's teenage spots rose through the lacto-calamine lotion and turned red as concentration on every phrase lit his face. He was probably nothing then without the PA system, but each utterance he dredged up was like a brushstroke on a sound-painting. Learning all the time, a sandpapery quiver during a dragged-out note with the microphone at arm's length could be as loaded as a roar with him almost swallowing it.

When he wasn't purposefully trying to mimic someone, he sounded like a cross between Slim Harpo[5] and the obscure Boogie Bill Webb, maker of just one single, 1952's Imperial release 'I Ain't For It', a disc that Jagger – expert though he'd become – was probably unaware of then. Yet there was also something else about Mick's overall effect on listeners. Attempting to get a handle on it, expatriate New Yorker Joe Boyd contended, 'Americans, if they sang blues, were obsessed with sounding like black men, whereas Mick showed them how to sing blues and be unashamed of being white and being a kind of tarty little English schoolboy. There wasn't the same awkwardness. It was a much more relaxed position towards shopping in different cultures among the English.'[6]

If his pitching of high notes was a bit hit or miss, a pimply herbert from the LSE – barely the Mannish Boy that Muddy Waters bragged about being – showed that you didn't have to come from the chain gang or the ghettos of southside Chicago to sound world-weary, cynical and knowing beyond your years. If you half-closed your eyes, with delicate suspension of logic, this stripling's bashed-about rasp would seem believable as, from a reserve of passion – however unsubstantiated – he would be putting on the agony three nights a week with Blues Incorporated at the Marquee – the National Jazz Federation's main London venue – as well as the G Club. One such appearance brought Jagger his earliest mention – and that's all it was – in the British music press.

Yet neither Jagger, Baldry nor Wood were singled out as a particularly integral part of the setup, often taking a literal back seat while awaiting their turn. 'Alexis didn't really want a singer who would take over the front line,' said Mick. 'It was like the old big bands, where you had the singer who would croon a couple of numbers, and then the "real thing" would happen and the band leader would take over.'[7]

This policy was echoed in a faraway Sheffield establishment named Bluesville, which had its own Blues Incorporated in The Chuck Fowler R&B Band, while other provincial venues were also to turn into blues strongholds on off-peak evenings. Random examples are the R&B Club above Andover's Copper Kettle restaurant, where The Troggs began; Club Rado – which cradled Van Morrison's Them – in the Old Sailors' Maritime Dance Hall in Belfast; the Downbeat in Newcastle's dockland, where Eric Burdon hollered with what would metamorphose into The Animals; and, in a hostelry beneath the shadow of Birmingham Town Hall, Rhythm Unlimited, birthplace of The Spencer Davis Group on an occasion when, within an hour of its 7:30 start, over 80 latecomers had been turned away. 'The packed crowd at the opening session and subsequent evenings make it quite clear that there is a tremendous following for R&B in the city,'[8] crowed co-promoter Brian Allen.

In nearly all such places, the loudest applause was saved for the numbers on the frontier of rock 'n' roll, a fact not lost on Mick Jagger at the G Club: 'When Keith and I got up and did our two numbers, the crowd went bananas. It was quite obvious they liked that kind of music.'[7]

It was, however, expedient to deny that he sang anything other than strict R&B when, a few weeks after their G Club debut, he, Dick and Keith – all that was left of Little Boy Blue And The Blue Boys – joined forces with this Brian Jones bloke and a thick-set pianist from the East End named Ian Stewart, whose heart was in pre-war boogie-woogie but who was prepared to give Reed, Berry, Diddley and so forth a go.

There wasn't room for three guitarists, so Dick Taylor was persuaded by self-appointed leader Brian to switch to bass. When the myth gripped harder, it was said that Jones also chose the group's name from song titles on a Muddy Waters LP,[9] yet to his chagrin they were 'Mick Jagger's Rolling Stones' in a *Jazz News* article about 'eight R&B bands now in business' in London.[10]

Though he regarded The Rolling Stones as the laggards of the pack – largely because they lacked a permanent drummer – Harold Pendleton, the Marquee's manager, gave them an intermission spot 'while we all went for a drink. The club wasn't licensed then, so I never saw the Stones.'[3] However, unfavourable opinions about their authenticity – one from no less an authority than Chris Barber – caused Pendleton to stop booking them. 'They mucked about with things and played them faster, not like the records,' suggested Phil May, an art-school friend of Taylor and Richards. 'They didn't have the reverence for the form that Alexis Korner and all that high church of the Ealing club blues potentates had.'

Yet, for every door slammed on The Rolling Stones, others creaked pedantically ajar, and *Jazz News* soon reported that 'Mick Jagger and The Rolling Stones are touring the local clubs to appreciative audiences.'[10] The journal did not stress that, at some of these local clubs, 'opening night' meant 'final performance', convened as they were at the Stones' own expense, mostly in pub function rooms on the capital's southwestern fringes. On the day of one such booking, there'd been a cold spell with heavy rain all day, as well as something good on television that evening. Apart from the five Stones, one of their transient drummers, the janitor and his barking dog, the hall had been completely empty.

4 Bright Lights, Big City

'Mick was great fun. He was absolutely so funny. Brian
could be quite serious at times, but Mick had his freedom;
he was at university; he was still living at home.'

– Pat Andrews

Over the weeks since the formation of the Stones, Mick had had
ample opportunity to log the characteristics of Brian Jones and
Ian Stewart. The latter was pleasant enough, and respected by
everyone for his reliability and steadiness, while the more nicely
spoken but volatile Brian was given to bouts of sulking and was
the most frequent originator of intrigues and discord within the
group – although this was mitigated by his aptitude for selling the
Stones to gruff landlords and wary entertainment secretaries.

Jones's cynical recoiling against a privileged upbringing
centred on the Church manifested itself in small ways, such as
the crooked smile that he directed at Dick Taylor when, one
evening at Wilmington, Joe Jagger said grace before the dinner
to which Jones, Taylor and Richards had been invited. Possibly
because he also suffered from emotional self-doubt, Jones – all
blond androgyny – was also a sexual braggart, even if some of
his paranoiac tales of women he'd not only seduced but
impregnated had substance. Currently, he was shacked up in
Notting Hill with a girl from back home in Cheltenham named
Pat Andrews and their infant son.

A jealous if faithless lover, Brian frowned when Pat said as
much as a civil hello to any male not on his mental list of those

who he deemed to have no romantic interest in her. Of the Stones, he was particularly anxious about Jagger – with sound reason, as it turned out – and his heart sank to his boots when, recalled Pat, 'Mick arrived at our place about four on a Friday morning on a summer's day when it was just turning light. He said that it was too late to get the milk train home. Could he stay the night? Brian wasn't happy about this, because he had to go to his day job when Mick was still asleep. He didn't want to go and leave Mick here with me.

'Mick woke up and I gave him a cup of tea. Then I sat on the settee where he'd slept, and he put his arm round me as if to give me a kiss. I get really embarrassed when people do that when I'm not expecting it, so I took it as a joke. Years later, a friend rang me to tell me that a book had come out in which Keith was quoted as saying that while Brian was at work, Mick screwed me. That definitely wasn't true.'

Whether or not some hint of this episode penetrated Brian's sensitive psyche, it may have been no coincidence that, shortly after it, Pat and the baby fled back to Cheltenham, and Brian was sharing Keith and Mick's flat at 102 Edith Grove, situated in World's End, a few streets too far from fashionable Chelsea. Jagger had had to jump the highest hurdle of parental opposition, but eventually Joe and Eva had supposed it was fair enough for him to fly the nest in August 1962, just before his second academic year at the LSE. If nothing else, it would lessen the chances of him being late for morning lectures.

Dick Taylor preferred to remain in Bexleyheath, confessing that he was 'slightly appalled by Edith Grove. It didn't exactly inspire me to leave home.' Each visit brought another squalid detail to light, whether the soiled newspaper unflushed in the stinking communal lavatory or a fresh avalanche of plaster that the door knocker's rapping thunder had dislodged from the hallway wall. In rooms an estate agent might describe as 'compact' was a coin-guzzling electricity meter, neglected household chores, body odour, undisguised greed at meal times and general unconcern about the state of the place. It was understood that as long as you didn't fall behind with the rent – most of which came from Jagger's grant cheque – you could revel in romantic squalor – well, squalor, anyway – get carried home drunk at seven in the morning, lie in until the streetlights came on, leave crockery unwashed in the sink and entertain persons of a different set of hormones behind the closed door of your bedroom.

For Mick, there was always the safety net of his tut-tutting mother's home cooking, the untaxing televisual comfort of *The Adventures Of Robin Hood* and *The Phil Silvers Show*, soft toilet tissue and constant hot water, which helped him get his nerve back to step over the puddle of vomit on number 102's stairwell, now giving life to some sort of fungus.

Worse, 1962's record-breaking winter chill struck Edith Grove like a hammer, accompanied initially by a windy drizzle that was almost but not quite a gale. Then snow fell, on and off, from December until the following so-called spring. Bickering helped pass the time, as did poking ruthless fun at whoever seemed likelier to rise to it (usually Brian). So, more constructively, did instrumental practice, which saw Mick wailing along on his harmonica as the Dansette was warmed up by rotations of *Muddy Waters At Newport* or *Folk Festival Of The Blues*, the latter from a concert the previous summer showcasing the cream of Chicago bluesmen.

If not up to Cyril Davies's self-protecting standard, Jagger was no slouch on harmonica these days, with other players – such as Rod Stewart, then a West End busker – learning what they could of his technique from below the lip of the stage, as it was then easy to get sufficiently close to make out whether Mick was blowing or sucking.

Although attendance figures had improved of late, prospects didn't seem rosy enough for Dick Taylor to continue as a Rolling Stone. 'The politics of everything changed after I left,' he would note. The democracy of old was replaced by an oligarchy of Jagger,

Jones and Richards, after Dick was replaced by Bill Wyman, a married father from south London who'd had a brush with fame in a backing group to Dickie Pride, a diminutive one-hit wonder whose voice rather than his face was his fortune – though his onstage convulsions had earned him the nickname 'the Sheik of Shake'. Jagger and Stewart were both cordial towards Wyman on first acquaintance, and the other two warmed to him because, like Charlie Watts – the former Blues Incorporated drummer who joined two months later in January – 'Bill didn't make waves,' Phil May suggested. 'He accepted that he wasn't in the inner sanctum and was OK about it.'

The newcomers' midwinter arrival correlated neatly with another sea-change in the Stones. On Sunday 27 January 1963, they began a weekly residency at the Craw Daddy in the capacious back room of Richmond's Station Hotel. Three weeks later, it was two-thirds full. The next Sunday, it was packed out. From then on, customers would queue up to three hours before the start. As well as the same blues aficionados who might also frequent the G Club, the Stones were luring aesthetes whose record collections might once have advertised a pseudo-sophistication that ran from Stravinsky to the most limp and 'tasteful' modern jazz, and whose skip-read Genet, Nietzsche, Camus and Sartre looked well on university hostel bookshelves.

In the Stones, the young (and generally male) intellectual detected a certain Neanderthal *épater le bourgeoisie* and received the knowledge that the group's more rugged brand of R&B was 'uncommercial', and thus an antidote to the contrived splendour of television pop stars. He'd tell his mates where he'd been, describing what happened at the Craw Daddy in awestruck detail and delighting in the faint revulsion that chased across their faces. However, not wishing to appear prudish, they'd go with him – with toffee noses asking to be punched – on his next visit to this low-life gala.

Yet, when the initial shock was over, they'd feel what he had felt. Losing a little of their cultivated cool, such visitors even began to have fun – or, at least, via some complex inner debate, gave in to a self-conscious conviviality – as they attuned to the situation's epic vulgarity. These Rolling Stones got to be quite addictive. Much of the Craw Daddy's attraction, too, was being studied (not always surreptitiously) by not just blue-stockings in glasses but also gaggles of short-skirted 'town girls', jabbering incessantly until the Stones sauntered onto the boards, downright uncouth in their verbal retaliations to shouted comments from the massed humanity bobbing up and down in the blackness. Hitting all their instruments at once at a staccato 'Right!' from the grotesque beauty addressed as 'Mick', they'd barge into a glorious onslaught of pulsating bass, dranging guitars, crashing drums and ranting vocals, walking what seemed to be a taut artistic tightrope without a safety net. Dammit, they were great!

Exuding all the breathy sentience of a man who'd been sprinting, this Mick character's sylph-like athlete's physique drew cow-eyed efforts to grab his attention from libidinous front-row females. 'If they couldn't get him, they'd go for the others,' observed Richard Hattrell, then the Stones' unofficial road manager. 'Surprisingly, many of them were aristocratic birds kicking up against their titled backgrounds and looking for excitement. It was sex for the sake of sex.'

'My whole act is made up from different girls I've been with,' the lad himself would joke later. 'I took the pout from Chrissie Shrimpton.'[1] This was a reference to the 17-year-old younger sister of Jean Shrimpton, an up-and-coming fashion model. An acquaintance of Rod Stewart, it had been Chrissie who'd told the struggling singer about the Stones after she and Mick had started walking out together, and she'd had a blink-and-you'll-miss-her role in a promotional film of the group in all their sweaty intensity, financed by Giorgio Gomelsky, the Craw Daddy's proprietor and – as far as he was concerned – their manager in all but name.

Footage that included overhauls of Reed's 'Baby, What's Wrong' and Diddley's 'Pretty Thing' assisted the passage of the Stones into hitherto impenetrable bastions such as Studio 51, London's oldest jazz venue, and Oxford Street's 100 Club – opened in 1942 as the Feldman Swing Club – which were now booking trad bands to support what were looking and sounding dangerously like pop groups. At such a recital, Chris Jagger had been amused that one trad ensemble had worked 'R&B' into its name. There were also glimpses of comedy when some *bona fide* native R&B outfits tried to emulate the Reeds, Harpos, Waterses and Wolves half a world away. Praise indeed for Jimmy Powell And The Five Dimensions was annotated in Berkshire bluesman Mike 'Drivin' Wheel' Cooper's diary: 'Powell is a reasonable harmonica player and vocalist. His rhythm guitarist is quite good, too. The rest of the group are mediocre but produce a competent sound which does at least sound like R&B and not rock.'

Give him credit, too, Billy Fury, a Perkin Warbeck to Dickie Pride's Lambert Simnel as a pretender to Cliff Richard's crown, was to stand as tall with Jimmy Reed's 'Baby What You Want Me To Do', B-side of 'It's Only Make Believe', his penultimate Top Ten entry.

A solo singer in an age of groups, Fury was drowning in the flood of chart-busting outfits from Merseyside and acts plundered by London talent scouts from other regions during a search for further two-guitars-bass-drums archetypes of the British beat explosion, spearheaded by The Beatles and others under the aegis of Brian Epstein, once a sales manager in a Liverpool department store. Though Decca had already issued 'Sugar Babe' by Jimmy Powell And His Five Dimensions,[2] generally regarded as the first 'Brumbeat' single, what the label was after ideally was either a new Beatles or an *anti*-Beatles, because, after waving a cheery goodbye on ventriloquist dummy Lenny The Lion's show on BBC TV's *Children's Hour*, it wouldn't have seemed all that peculiar if the Fab Four had been shoe-shuffling next. 'It registered subconsciously,' thought Andrew Loog Oldham, one of Epstein's publicists, 'that when they made it, another section of the public was going to want the opposite.'[3]

Far from being fun for all the family, The Rolling Stones were being groomed as devils to The Beatles' angels by Gomelsky, who had cajoled *Record Mirror*'s Norman Jopling to pen a glowing review. 'The paper's policy was only to write about people who had records out,' Jopling elucidated, 'but there was such a buzz about them that Peter Jones, the editor, told me to go ahead. What amazed me – because I was a huge Bo Diddley fan – was that they could replicate his raw sound. I'd never seen a British band that came anywhere near that. My feature appeared on 11 May 1963, but *Record Mirror* was on the streets three days earlier, and immediately three of the four major British record labels – Philips, Decca and EMI – were on the phone to me. They all wanted to know where they could contact The Rolling Stones.'[4]

The telephone number Jopling gave them was not Gomelsky's but that of Andrew Loog Oldham, who'd seized the reins of the Stones' management while the hapless Giorgio was at his father's funeral in Switzerland. 'During the discussions, they didn't mention Gomelsky,' shrugged Oldham. 'Really, I think they were stringing him along.'[4]

At 16, Oldham had been taken on as a general assistant-*cum*-window dresser in Bazaar, a Knightsbridge boutique owned by Mary Quant, Jean Shrimpton's *haute couture* Diaghilev. Three years later, in 1963, after discovering a flair for publicity in Quant's employ, he found himself 'doing public relations on a freelance basis for some Brian Epstein acts. Contrary to popular opinion, I wasn't looking for something else to do. I was a very happy man. One day, I went to see Peter Jones of *Record Mirror*. He kept talking about this group called The Rolling Stones, playing around London.'[4]

There remains bitter division about Oldham. Was he an imaginative and overgrown boy sucked into a vortex of circumstances he was unable to resist, one of the cleanest new brooms ever to sweep the pop industry, or an English edition of conniving and manipulative Sergeant Bilko, living on his wits in *The Phil Silvers Show*?

If the latter was the case, the Colonel Hall to Andrew's Bilko was Eric Easton, 17 years his senior, who, if steeped in the traditions and lodged conventions of British showbusiness, was respected and liked by his many prestigious clients, not least because he aspired once to be an entertainer himself. However, Eric accepted that his time in the spotlight was up and that solid cash was preferable to public acclamation. Since the 1950s, he'd amassed enough connections in the industry to make a living behind the scenes, eventually forming his own agency – one that was concerned more than others with the long-term development of its artists. As Oldham's partner, he'd attempted to instil into the ramshackle Stones the 'professionalism' he'd perceived in those on his books who traded in 'decent music', but succeeded chiefly in amusing the six of them with his name-dropping and endless anecdotes about showbiz days past.

His principal gripe about the group was that they'd already failed a BBC audition because Mick sounded 'too coloured'. He went further: Jagger 'couldn't sing' – not 'real singing' like Roy Orbison's cowboy operatics or Presley when he tackled 'quality' material like his idol, Dean Martin. What Eric had to admit, however, was that Mick had 'image', and that he and the Stones 'were producing this fantastic sound that was obviously exactly right for the kids'.[4]

He was also in complete agreement with Andrew that some way would have to be found to tell Ian Stewart that he couldn't be a visible member of the Stones any more, although he could still be part of the team, albeit as more a glorified road manager than a musician. Why? 'He looked a bit like my Dad, who was a boxer,' smiled Dick Taylor. 'Ian was a big bloke with a big face.' While he'd always feel entitled to refer to the Stones as *us* rather than *them*, Stewart's widow was to insist that, 'Whatever Ian or anyone else said, he did care about being relegated. The bottom line for Andrew was that his face didn't fit. Andrew loved the pretty, thin, long-haired boys. Ian felt bitter about the savage way he was kicked aside.'[4]

The boot hadn't yet been drawn back when Easton and Oldham were mulling over strategies for gaining a recording contract. As The Beatles were proving too lucrative an investment for EMI, they decided to target its chief competitor, Decca. The previous year, Dick Rowe, the label's head recording manager, had auditioned and rejected The Beatles, considering them no better or worse than any other guitar group who conjured up back-of-beyond youth clubs with soft drinks, ping-pong and a presiding curate who, like Rowe, was then unaware of the faraway commotion in the north.

Setting aside his critical prejudices, therefore, Dick donned dark glasses and took his wife to the Craw Daddy. Consequent negotiations with Easton and the much less co-operative Oldham delivered The Rolling Stones to Decca. They were to prove the biggest post-Beatles fish to be hooked by Rowe, eclipsing even Brian Poole And The Tremeloes, then racing up the Top 20 with their fifth single. Poole would remember a joint photo shoot with the newly contracted Stones when 'our fan-club secretary came in with a load of photographs for us to sign, and Mick said, "You'd never catch me doing that. I'd have a rubber stamp made." Not long after that, the Stones became Decca's blue-eyed boys.'

5 The Moon Is Rising

'Wake up in the morning, there's a pop that really says,
"Rice Krispies for you and you and you…"'
– Mick Jagger[1]

The most immediate problem facing the Stones was the A-side
of a maiden single. With a plentiful internal source of self-penned
items, courtesy of John Lennon and Paul McCartney, The Beatles
were giving the music-publishing firms of Denmark Street –
London's Tin Pan Alley – a nasty turn, but the demarcation line
between composer and artiste persisted still, and the Stones
didn't intend to challenge it. Consolidation rather than progress
was the watchword then. 'We do not use any original material,'
Mick Jagger had told *Jazz News*. 'After all,' he added blithely,
'can you imagine a British composed R&B number? It just
wouldn't make it.'[2]

Grubbing around metropolitan publishers' offices was,
therefore, out of the question. There was no other alternative but
to rifle the vaults of the US motherlode. By process of elimination,
this boiled down to the songs of Chuck Berry – whose material
dominated the Stones' stage set – and those of countless other
beat groups. As simultaneous covers of the same number was not
unusual then, this narrowed the choice further, and after discarding
'Roll Over, Beethoven' (just issued by Pat Wayne And His
Beachcombers on EMI) and 'Around And Around' (which had
B-sided Berry's million-selling 'Johnny B Goode'), they settled on
an opus attractive for its unpopularity amongst rivals and which

would thus ensure a clear run. Nobody else did 'Come On', but, speeded up, it was quite danceable.

The Stones themselves dropped it from their repertoire after they agreed to mime 'Come On' in aberrant uniform attire on ITV's Saturday-evening pop show *Thank Your Lucky Stars*, sending it on its way to Number 21 in the charts. For first-timers, this was no mean achievement, and its very release on 7 June 1963 was sufficient motivation for Jagger to write to Kent Education Committee – the providers of his grant – terminating his course at the LSE. He portrayed it as a 'sabbatical' to his parents but as boat-burning to those Dartford Grammar cronies with whom he'd stayed in touch. An appalled Peter Holland, now at the nearby University College, would recall 'him telling me he was now singing in a group. I really laughed. "What do you mean, singing?" I said, "You haven't got a voice."'[3]

Joe and Eva, however, held on hoping that it wouldn't be too late for him to resume his degree studies, heartened as they were by his remarks in the *New Musical Express* about the wretched group being 'an enjoyable pastime. We consider ourself professional amateurs',[4] and, to *Melody Maker*, 'I know this won't last. I give the Stones another two years. I'm saving for the future.'[5] Making the most of his estimated time in the limelight, he seemed not only to take the pert *Thank Your Lucky Stars* outfits in his stride but would also submit to soundtracking an ITV commercial for a breakfast cereal, and be amenable to endorsing a Dickie Pride-esque gimmick in a head-tossing at the microphone that sections of the Craw Daddy audience copied.

'It gets so crowded that all fans can do is stand and twitch,' he elucidated. 'They can't dance because there isn't room.'[6] Expediently, Jagger's actions also resembled not so much a dance as a mass tic known as the Twitch, propagated briefly as one of many alternatives to the Twist, still going strong in 1963. There was even a Twitch Club in Birmingham whose house band, The Rockin' Berries, had immortalised the dance on an eponymous 1963 B-side.

Knowingly and unknowingly, Mick demonstrated the Twitch on a round of ballroom one-nighters, often setting off with just a contact's telephone number on a scrap of paper and, nearing journey's end, looking out for posters to see where and at what time they were on. The jaunt took the Stones to agricultural and factory towns where the 1950s wouldn't end until about 1966. Confronted with the Edith Grove contingent's hair now curtaining their faces, like Beatle moptops gone to seed – and Bill and Charlie not far behind – young adults in the sticks were just as shocked as their elders. A bunch of them might be relaxing over a game of darts in the pub:

'Mine's a Guinness. Double six to win, isn't it? What about that lot on at the Corn Exchange, eh? The band room's like a ponces' parlour.'

'Yeah, and they make a terrible row into the bargain. Don't look now but three of 'em have just walked into the lounge bar.'

'Hello! The landlord's refusing to serve 'em. I don't blame him. Get a load of that cissy heading for the gents'. Wrong one, mate!'

Yet, when watching like lynxes as the Stones loaded their equipment after the performance, antagonistic local cowboys would deduce that these aliens weren't cissies. Indeed, they were very much the opposite; limbering up for another long haul back to London, at least one of them might be against the shadowed side of the van, pawing some available girl. Coming on as the rough, untamed East Ender, Jagger in particular was discovering that a fledgling pop star's life brought more than mere money, but with the condition, 'Ugh! We used to attract such big, ugly ones. Dreadful birds with long, black hair, plastic boots and macs.'[7]

Jagger would sense being observed with interest by males, too, not always hostile or cissy. At a village institute somewhere in the eastern shires, one ogling female's nose was put out of joint when Jagger, overlooking her, introduced himself to her escort and chatted to him about the current state of pop. The boy was Syd Barrett, awaiting his destiny with The Pink Floyd, who were to begin in 1965 with a familiar dipping into the Waters, Diddley and Berry songbooks.

Among future chart contenders who owed not a little to the Stones' source material were The Kinks (despite trying to catch earlier lightning with two Merseybeat-tinged singles for Pye), The Downliners Sect (who became to Studio 51 what the Stones had been to the Craw Daddy) and The Yardbirds, Jagger *et al*'s successors at the latter venue, who would stray further than either the Sect or the Stones from their R&B core.

More directly involved as he was, Dick Taylor was pleased that his old colleagues had 'come on a lot' at the Craw Daddy, but the entry of 'Come On' into the Top 50 on 25 July 1963 was a confusing moment for him. A secret relief at departing the shabbiest nook of showbusiness imaginable gave way to reflection that the rewards of being in an R&B outfit might now extend beyond beer money and a laugh. Like others much less qualified, therefore, Taylor formed a group – named The Pretty Things, after a Bo Diddley number – that invited inevitable comparisons, not all of them flattering. Mike Cooper wrote in his diary that the singer, Phil May, was 'a sickening effigy of Mick Jagger. The Stones have just succeeded in making a name for themselves, and already some maniac, an anaemic-looking little punk, is on his tail.'

Yet, united by artistic purpose and mutual respect, there was much camaraderie between the Stones and the groups that followed in their wake, with Jagger clambering on stage at the Marquee to sing 'Bright Lights, Big City' with The Yardbirds' Keith Relf; Phil May borrowing Mick's book containing handwritten lyrics of 'every Chuck Berry, every Bo Diddley, every Jimmy Reed song'; and Mick admitting that he found Phil's offhand stagecraft instructive. Jagger also noted the spasmodic crouching and jumping about of Paul Jones, now lead vocalist with Manfred Mann, recently appointed to pen a new theme for ITV's new pop showcase *Ready Steady Go* and coming up with '54321', a catchy if self-mythologising opus that reached the Top Ten before it was even heard on the programme.

The Stones had yet to make such a breakthrough when, on their first national tour, Jagger was diligent in making private observations of one of the headlining acts' performances for incorporation into his own. In the previous year, Little Richard's show had been a gospel revue in keeping with his enrolment at theological college and a subsequent ministry, but it had become a straight rock 'n' roll show by the time it reached Europe, albeit trading 'heys' and 'yeahs' with his audiences like glory-bound preacher–congregation interplay. 'He drove the whole house into a complete frenzy,' marvelled Mick. 'It's hypnotic, like an evangelistic meeting.'[8]

Quite a few ticket-holders mustered up louder screams for the Stones than for Richard and The Everly Brothers – white North Americans on the bill – particularly as the duo's last three 45s had fought shyer of the Top 20 than 'Come On'. Furthermore, the Stones were buoyed towards the end of the trek by the impending release of its follow-up, 'I Wanna Be Your Man', picked to click by an *NME* reviewer after it had been tossed to them by Lennon and McCartney, as the two Beatles had tossed hits earlier in 1963 to fellow Merseysiders Billy J Kramer, The Fourmost and Cilla Black.

Described in one *New Musical Express* feature as 'a London group with the Liverpool sound',[4] the Stones were still being pigeonholed for convenience as a southern wing of fast-fading Merseybeat as late as spring 1964, when a third 45 – an arrangement of 'Not Fade Away', the Buddy Holly number that had besotted Jagger and Dick Taylor in 1958 – slipped into the Top Ten midway through an all-British package tour. The running order of the presentation was subject to change after John Leyton, Mike Sarne, Billie Davis and Mike Berry – all with a backlog of hits but no current entry in the Top 40 – were each upstaged by the Stones and, to a smaller degree, The Swinging Blue Jeans, now that the swing towards beat groups was complete.

On the Little Richard trek, the Stones had never been certain that they'd sleep in proper beds each night. Because Brian stayed with his parents at the Cheltenham stop, the budget could be stretched for the others to put up at the town's Irving Hotel – where, incidentally, Mick sang with the resident Tony Faye and his Fayetones while Keith, Bill, Charlie and Ian held court in the bar. These days, however, the Stones couldn't afford *not* to book accommodation in advance now that darkness was their sole shield against the havoc that would accumulate around them. It was no longer possible for any of them to take the air after breakfast without public fuss.

Not so much famous now as notorious, 'the caveman-like quintet'[9] had been threatened with an ITV ban for 'unprofessional conduct' after rolling up two hours late for a final run-through for *The Arthur Haynes Show*,[10] a prime-time comedy series with musical interludes. Then there were priggish restauranteurs at pains to point out that any male not wearing a tie wasn't to be served lunch; auditorium janitors promising to pull the main electricity switch the second that the group's horrible racket over-ran; and night porters unwilling to leave desks unattended to prepare sandwiches when the silly little twerps flopped in after the show. The sign says you're to hand them room keys in when you go out. Can't you read? No, I don't suppose you can.

Mick might take challenging books in order to occupy idle hours lying fully clothed on cheap hotel beds. However, it would occur to him that he'd scarcely peeked at a solitary page during the entire trip. Sometimes, the highlight of the day wasn't the show but the building up, the winding down and the roguish pranks played when other acts were on. At the ABC Cinema, Stockton-on-Tees, where The Spencer Davis Group would be among the support acts, Mick would spread cold chips on the blind side of singer Steve Winwood's piano – not that the effect was noticed amid the tumult.

In readiness for the evening's screaming at the Stones, girls getting used to mini-skirts may have trimmed newly styled fringes with nail clippers in order 'to identify with these characters as either other girls or as sexual neuters',[11] as one psychiatrist wrote.

This may have been why all-boys schools like Dartford Grammar had become especially strict about short hair as a mark of sobriety and masculinity. It also labelled those who didn't mind it as supportive of a kind of official, malevolent neutrality towards intellectually stultifying pop groups, who – compounding their infamy – were now inclined to gesture with cigarettes and let loose the odd mild but un-Cliff Richard-like expletive like *crap* and *bloody* during television interviews and press conferences.

Outside school, however, beat music was gaining ground. Top 20 selections were heard over the PA at Tottenham Hotspur's soccer pitch. The Dave Clark Five's early hits were particularly popular there, for not only had local lad Dave called his publishing company Spurs Music but he was also leader of a group with a sporty outlook, as shown in the keep-fit scene that would open their 1965 celluloid vehicle, *Catch Us If You Can*.[12]

This was much at odds with the effeminate aura radiating from the likes of The Rolling Stones – 'the Five Shaggy Dogs with a brand of "shake" all their own', as one local rag had it[13] – and, indeed, hair was the primary cause of blazing rows between parents and once tractable sons. If he could get away with it, a boy might approximate a Brian Jones feather-duster cut or try to look like someone who looked like Mick, whose appearance was chief among reasons why Bob Geldof – then a Dublin teenager – identified with 'The Rolling Stones, the first band I considered my own. Mick Jagger's hair was a mess, and my hair was a mess, even when it was short.'[14]

Yet Jagger visited the barber's more frequently than Geldof may have assumed, having his hair cut 'not short, but regularly'.[15] A statement that some took as vague defence had come from a Mr Scowcroft, president of the National Hairdressers' Federation: 'Men's hairdressers do not object to youth wanting to wear its hair long, provided it is shaped.'[16]

Men don't have periods and can't get pregnant, but pillars of Women's Lib might note how difficult the issue of hair could be in the 1960s for boys who had to fight every literal inch of the way against being as humiliated and degraded beneath a barber's clippers as many a village patriarch in Tzarist Russia had been when punished by the removal of his flowing patriarchal beard.

No amount of backcombing, pulling or application of a thickening gel called *Dippety-Do* could disguise your shearing at a time when a BBC producer refused to allow a vocalist to appear on television until he'd had his shoulder-length locks abbreviated and 11 boys were suspended from a Coventry secondary school for having 'Mick Jagger' haircuts. An editorial in a tabloid newspaper advocated a law that made short-back-and-sides cuts compulsory for men, and a nasty rumour filtered around provincial Britain about Jagger's impending sex-change. 'They are not looked on very kindly by most parents or by adults in general,' observed the *Daily Mirror*. 'They are even used to the type of article that asks big brother if he would let his sister go out with one of them.'[17]

As well as looking like trouble, the Stones made trouble, eventually notching up more court appearances than any other British pop group. On 27 November 1964, Jagger would be convicted of his second driving offence in six months. This time, his counsel's plea led to a not-altogether-relevant discussion, to be later reiterated in a schoolgirls' comic: 'The Emperor Augustus Caesar was another with long hair [*sic*], and he won a great many victories. Put out of your mind the nonsense talked about these young men. These boys are highly intelligent, not long-haired idiots, as some people care to refer to them. Mick's shaggy mane is a Grade A asset to Britain.'[18]

6 Tell The World I Do

'The fantasy is driving around in a big car, having all the chicks you want and being able to pay for it. It always has been, always will be.'

– Mick Jagger[1]

Although the Stones had scratched the surface of North America four months earlier, the international campaign really began in France, specifically at the Paris Olympia on an October Tuesday in 1964 when the group worked up their customary pandemonium. This time, however, it was a majority of boys who were worked into a froth, their rioting spilling out onto the boulevards.

Attending all three shows, 19-year-old Françoise Hardy – pictured by indolent domestic columnists as a new Juliette Gréco – took advantage of a photo opportunity with the group and figured in plans (which came to nothing) for her and Mick Jagger to star in a remake of Jean Cocteau's *Les Enfants Terribles*. With a fellow *chanteuse* adopting the stage alias 'Stone', and much-televised combo Les Problèmes mirroring their coiffeur and musical style, the Stones were arguably ahead of The Beatles not only in France but also everywhere else in continental Europe.

Just as The Beatles had thought it opportune to record German-language versions of certain of their hits, so the Stones released an Italy-only single, 'Con Le Mie Lacrime' – a translation of 'As Tears Go By', one of the first fruits of the Jagger–Richards songwriting team. Belying Mick's earlier assertion about the Stones' disinclination to try self-penned material, one such opus, 'Tell Me' – admittedly as far from Jimmy Reed and Chuck Berry as it could be – was selected for the group's eponymous debut long-player to a response ranging from the *NME*'s 'a sad song which will compel people to really listen to the words'[2] to *Melody Maker*'s in-house grumpy old man Bob Dawburn cold-shouldering it as 'second-hand Liverpool'.[3]

Mick and Keith's breaking cover as composers was down to Andrew Oldham's steady drip of incitement, bringing up the subject each time they spoke – which was frequently, as the three were now sharing a west Hampstead flat eminently more comfortable than 102 Edith Grove. One immediate result of his nagging, 'My Only Girl', was recorded by the otherwise unsung George Bean, but was remoulded as 'That Girl Belongs To Yesterday' by Gene Pitney, a visiting US singer who, for all his smart, besuited image, was breathing the air around The Rolling Stones.

1963's '24 Hours From Tulsa' had been Pitney's first big British strike, after one of that year's predecessors, 'Mecca', had been issued too late to prevent a cover by The Cheetahs – a unit from a Birmingham suburb – from snatching the slight chart honours. While 'That Girl Belongs To Yesterday' restored Gene to the Top Ten, its exploration of the same area as 'Tell Me' compounded the stereotyping of him as a merchant of melancholy.

During conversations with him in idle moments during sessions for the Stones' natal album, Jagger came to understand that Gene was respected within the pop industry because, while advised by managers and other payroll courtiers, he was no corporation marionette in an age when so many other stars – especially in North America – seemed devoid of independent opinion about career development and the piffle they were given to sing. Although he made doubtful decisions over the years, Pitney alone accepted responsibility for them. Indeed, he maintained an intense and often unwelcome interest in every link of the chain, from studio to pressing plant to market place.

Mick would remember his informal lessons in the tricks of the trade from Gene, who, mixing work with pleasure, was to be romantically linked with Marianne Faithfull, a filly whom Oldham had just added to his managerial stable. She was what George Bernard Shaw might have called a 'downstart', in that she came from a family that had once been better off. Marianne dwelt with her mother – a lady of Austrian aristocratic stock – at 12 Milman Road in Reading and attended St Joseph's Convent School, opposite the local university and known parochially as 'Holy Joe's'. She walked to her lessons along the main thoroughfare that divided the student district from Whitley, the most forlorn suburb of the Berkshire county town, reckoned by makers of television documentaries to be the most 'average' in Britain.

By her A-level year at Holy Joe's, the blonde sixth-former had become a leading light of amateur-dramatic productions at the nearby Progress Theatre and was omnipresent – as was Mike Cooper – singing in floor spots at parochial folk clubs. John Dunbar, her 'steady', was at Cambridge and was consistent with her liking for 'tall men with glasses'.[4] In cold print, Marianne was as wholesome a Swinging '60s teenager as could be visualised on the cover of a schoolgirls' annual that balanced pop and fashion with features on pets, badminton, ballet, ponies and making a lampshade: conventionally beautiful and dancing in a not-too-way-out mid-calf dress with a short-haired boy, her eyes not focused on him.

To round things off, university beckoned, although she'd confess, 'I'm no egghead. What I really want to do eventually is settle down and get married'[5] – presumably to John, a Londoner, who was friends with Peter Asher, brother of Paul McCartney's then-girlfriend and half of Peter and Gordon, who had just entered the charts with a song penned for them by John Lennon and Paul.

In with the innermost in-crowd of all, Dunbar showed off Marianne at a launch party for 'Shang A Doo Lang', a Jagger–Richards opus and the second Decca single by Adrienne Posta, who had been at stage school with Steve Marriott. Marianne was introduced to the disc's producer, Andrew Loog Oldham, who saw pop-star potential in her cultured loveliness.

Proving Oldham's judgement to be correct, Marianne took 'As Tears Go By' into the British and, eventually, US charts, aided by an image – not completely assumed – of a posh and rather scatty provincial maid, amused if bewildered by her sudden fame. Gosh, who'd have thought it? Here's me, the hugest fan of Jane Austen, but a pop star! We're not all fuddy-duddies. Far from it! Just look at me: I wear mini-skirts now, and I'm pretty much the swingingest chick in Reading. I just happen to be a baroness's daughter who uses long words. Hey, I suppose I'm just mad, me!

The demo of the wan 'As Tears Go By' was just a session guitarist picking arpeggios behind Jagger, who was extraordinary to Marianne only as a spotty youth whose tearful girlfriend had been shouting at him at the Adrienne Posta do. Apparently, they were always rowing. Andrew said that, when he first came to investigate the Stones at the Craw Daddy, 'as I walked down an alley to the entrance at the back, this couple in the alley were having a very loud lovers' tiff. I just said, "Excuse me," and went past. It wasn't until Jagger came on stage that I realised that it had been him outside, and the girl was Chrissie Shrimpton.'[6]

John and Marianne's disagreements were nowhere as public – not that they were together much during the first flush of her stardom; he was hitch-hiking around Greece when Marianne was screen-testing for a movie and having Brian Epstein rubbing his chin and wondering if she was 'the Edith Piaf of the future'.[7] Finally, she put her faith in Andrew Oldham, trusting him to steer her through the sly quagmires of the entertainment business.

Between record dates and television plugs, she would be busy with round-Britain expeditions with the likes of The Hollies, Freddie And The Dreamers, Gene Pitney, Cliff Bennett And His Rebel Rousers, The Rockin' Berries, Gerry And The Pacemakers, Roy Orbison, The Kinks and the low-billed Manish Boys, the latter fronted by the fellow destined to be David Bowie. Dressing-room scenes were often quite irreproachably cosy, with Marianne maybe with her nose in *Sense And Sensibility* until Roy dropped by for a chat and, smiling indulgently, allowed himself to be photographed after a giggling Marianne removed his trademark sunglasses, and Jon Mark – her sole accompanist – tuning his acoustic guitar before making himself scarce with Orbison while she put her glad rags and make-up on.

Orbison, however, was drawn into the ribald mirth concerning his drummer's frustrated tilting for the downfall of Faithfull's knickers throughout an entire three-week tour. Moreover, Marianne was not the pretty innocent her more susceptible fans might have imagined; beyond simply smiling quietly at dirty jokes resounding from the back seat of the bus, her fling with Gene Pitney wasn't the only occasion on which she cuckolded – if that is the word – her on–off boyfriend, whose overseas activities might in any case have involved more than just sight-seeing and sunbathing. According to Paul Gadd, *Ready Steady Go*'s floor manager, her relationship with Mike Leander – the designated producer of 'As Tears Go By' – 'was something more than professional. At times, it got a bit complicated, and there was always a lot of whispering when Marianne was there.'[8]

Knowing looks were exchanged, too, about Marianne and a married member of The Hollies, while other rumours – including one about her and Mick Jagger – had grown from instances of simple flirting and, possibly, the other party's broadcasted all-lads-together fantasies. 'She was constantly prick-teasing everyone,' was the indelicate summary of Dave Davies, The Kinks' lead guitarist. 'All the guys boasted about how they'd had sex with her. She would sit on the coach with her lips puckered and her fake Sloane accent [*sic*] intact. I think she was really quite shy.'[9]

Marianne's private sweetness remained apparent to John Dunbar on his return from Greece, when his proposal of marriage was accepted. Within a year, Marianne was a married mother living in Knightsbridge, where their social circle was wide enough for an uneasy embrace of both showbusiness types and her husband's undergraduate pals.

Mick Jagger was on the periphery of Mrs Dunbar's life then, even as his *amour* with the volcanic Chrissie deteriorated, mortified as she was by 'friends' and press gossip informing her of the Stones' supposed satyric exploits when away from wives and loved ones. It was no longer humorous that the kind of girls who were proud of love-bites had nicknamed him Mick *Shagger*.

Quite what any of them would have done had she succeeded in shoving a hand through a gap in the wall of bodies mobbing the Stones to grab the belt of Shagger's trousers and pull is open to debate. Contrary to popular opinion, a bill-topping male on the 'scream circuit' then could but seldom tempt even the most ecstatic bird in the audience to join him for tea and biscuits in the green room. In his autobiography, the late Adam Faith recalled numerous episodes of directing his road manager to bring him someone who'd taken his fancy from the footlights, but receiving only her relayed message that he could get lost. What sort of girl did Adam Faith think she was? There was a difference, it seemed, between the distant object who had enslaved his audience and the mere mortal who picked his nose just like everybody else.

Mick was more disposed to try it on with female artists on any given tour, unafraid of being repulsed, as he was by Margo Lewis of Goldie and the Gingerbreads. 'She almost punched his head off his neck,' gasped the group's guitarist, Carol MacDonald. '"Who do you think you are? How dare you!" – because he thought he's the star so he could do that.'[10]

He didn't have much luck either with Twinkle, another Decca signing, whose journalist sister Dawn's nepotistic pieces in *Mirabelle*, *Jackie* and similar periodicals, and a spot on *Thank Your Lucky Stars* had helped to guide the 16-year-old's first 45, 'Terry', to Number Four. Of the same nicely spoken kidney as Marianne Faithfull, the erstwhile Lyn Annette Ripley's refined background remained detectable to the public, but, as she explained, 'I didn't have an image made up for me by a publicity department. All you saw was what I was. I'm very rebellious, and I was terribly anxious to get in with the fast crowd.' It made sense, therefore, for Mr and Mrs Ripley to insist on the offstage presence of a uniformed nanny to guard their daughter's chastity when Twinkle was engaged as an opening act for The Rolling Stones during four dates in Ireland in 1965's rainy September.

Twinkle had a taste of what they were like at a soundcheck in an auditorium a short drive from her Surrey home. 'A slight, pale youth was playing a guitar, and another guy with a mop of bright hair was effing and blinding at the top of his voice. "That fucking sound isn't right, Brian. It's too tacky. The whole noise is fucking crap!" He was very vulgar.

'Our footsteps were muted on the red carpet, and we'd climbed the few steps to the stage before anyone saw we were there. Dawn pulled me forward. "This is my sister, Twinkle," she said, "and don't let me ever hear you swear in front of her again. Twink, this is Mick Jagger."

'Faded blue eyes peeped from behind a scruffy fringe, and a rather small, freckled hand was outstretched. "Hello, Wink," he said, "or should it be 'Wank'?" I smiled. I know that it is hard to believe now, but neither Dawn nor I knew the meaning of the word "wank".'

Young Bob Geldof, sneaking into a Dublin theatre just after the Stones arrived for their first show in Ireland, was similarly taken aback to hear Jagger curse vilely, not realising that it was a pose at deliberate odds to the intrinsic decency of his upbringing. Twinkle had no reason either to assume that he was anything other than a toilet-talking lout, a rough diamond at best, when, after the show the following evening in Belfast, 'he grabbed my arm backstage. "Come with me," he said, "wherever you want to go."

'"To my bed. Alone," I replied.

'"Silly cow," he laughed. "I had Marianne Faithfull last week. She enjoyed it. Why not give it a try?" I declined his offer.

'After I closed my act the next night, Mick begged me to go out front. "I've got a ticket," he said. "I want to sing you a special song." Out of inquisitiveness, I took up his offer, and sat in the middle of the front row. He dedicated "If You Need Me" to me. It was a romantic moment, and after the gig, somewhere in the bowels of the theatre, he kissed me. It was a strange feeling, and I didn't like it much.

'As we left, and battled through thousands of fans, a girl tore at the top of my hair, leaving me with a one-inch spiky corridor. "Keep away from my Mick," she bawled. Nevertheless, when I got back home, I found time to rush out and buy the EP with "If You Need Me" on it and play it endlessly on repeat. I even took it to bed with me. Oh well, I was only human, Mick.'

A lady who would later succumb more perceptibly to Jagger's allure was Anita Pallenberg, whose main source of income at the time was as an actress in continental movies. On the rebound from a long affair with Mario Schifano, a visual-arts jack of all trades, she had been 'getting into rock 'n' roll'[11] when a Swedish photographer friend took her to meet the Stones in Munich not long after their return from Ireland – and not long before she moved in with Brian Jones.

Two years earlier, she and Schifano had been berthed on a ship bound for New York when President Kennedy had been assassinated on the same day that British pop papers proclaimed The Beatles' pending US trip the following February. Some would predicate that the consequent British Invasion of North America was an antidote to the depressing Christmas that had followed the shooting. Offering a more forthright theory, John Lennon opined, 'Kids everywhere go for the same thing and, seeing as we'd done it in England, there's no reason why we couldn't do it over there too.'[12]

North America's wonderment at all things British peaked in that 1964 week when The Beatles occupied *nine* positions in the Canadian Top Ten. Yet the British Invasion as a phenomenon had had less to do with the musicians themselves than with the behaviour of a public who, once convinced of something incredible, exhibited a fanaticism for it that left the British themselves swallowing dust.

The Stones were relatively slow to gain ground in North America. However, during the interval between their first and second visits, two releases – 'Tell Me', as a US-only single, and, 'It's All Over Now', their first UK Number One – each climbed to between Numbers 20 and 30 in the *Billboard* Hot 100. More insidiously, they amassed grassroots support epitomised by myriad Anglophile garage bands, who – with dubious musical ability clashing with overweening expressive ambition – borrowed from the Stones' dialectic, most blatantly by employing vocalists who could ape Mick's stentorian drawl and side-on mic stance, broken by handclaps above the head (when he wasn't either blowing his mouth organ or wielding maracas) and kicking one leg backwards, as if dancing a half-hearted Charleston.

Jagger added considerably to his arsenal of physical gyrations when the Stones were among many other weavers of the rich tapestry of mid-1960s pop participating in the Teen-Age Music International (TAMI) show at Santa Monica Auditorium in November 1964. Purportedly, he smoked an entire packet of apprehensive cigarettes as the group's allotted time approached. His nervousness wasn't just because it was being filmed for posterity; he was consigned to be preceded by James Brown, melodramatic and high-energy dean of soul music. Watching Brown hurl a hand-mic into the air, swivel around, do the splits, jump upright and catch it in the space of two effortless seconds would have cowed any callow beat-group singer, chart-riding and frantic, waiting in the wings and pondering how long his entrance could be delayed in order to allow the Brown-inflamed crowd to cool down.

Yet, typifying the underlying affability of pop's most optimistic period, James deigned to join the assembled cast for a finale centred on the Stones, and was to be most courteous when Jagger and Richards were conducted into his backstage presence at the Harlem Apollo, which, in macrocosm, was to Brown as the Craw Daddy had been to his callers. 'They were standing there like scared teenagers,' remembered Ronnie Spector of The Ronettes. 'They introduced themselves. He shook their hands, and that's all there was to it. I don't think James even knew who these weird English guys were, but Mick and Keith were practically shaking.'[13]

Later, Brown would protest that he brought Jagger onto the stage and introduced him to the Apollo's black audience; that the Stones 'got over real good' at the TAMI spectacular, and that he thought of them as 'brothers'.[14] That was after it became OK for the hippest of the US hip to dig the group. Frank Zappa, leader of the far-out Mothers Of Invention, was to choose an affectionate burlesque of Jagger for the lead vocal of 'Trouble Comin' Every Day' on his 1966 *Freak Out!* album, while protest singer-in-transition Bob Dylan hung out with Brian Jones and was pleased to hear that Mick preferred his rendition of 'The House Of The Rising Sun' to The Animals' million-selling version, and had derided as 'phoney' Barry McGuire's all-purpose 'Eve Of Destruction', *the* hit song of 1965, when protest was all the rage. The fact that Jagger believed Dylan was 'good but too fashionable to stay as popular as he is'[15] was a back-handed compliment of sorts.

The Stones were also clasped to the metaphorical bosom of Andy Warhol, ruler of New York's downtown Factory, an arts laboratory hinged on his mannered revelling in consumerism, mass-production and the emptiness of glamour, and a tacit mission statement to bring humour and topicality back into art via the earnest superficiality of soup-cans, Brillo pads, comic-strip philosophy, interesting-but-boring films like *Couch* and *Chelsea Girls* – and the mixed-media events that spawned The Velvet Underground, an outfit whose emotional vocabulary was to echo across the pop decades through an unprecedented coverage of drug addiction, sexual taboos and mental instability.

In the Big Apple, too, a hundred-foot-high illuminated portrait of the Stones in Times Square ensured a good turnout at a press conference to kick off their fourth North American tour in autumn 1965. It was alleged by local guitarist Lee Underwood that a freelance photographer named Linda Eastman spent the subsequent night with Jagger 'and wrote about it in an American teen magazine'.[16] If it ever existed, the article in question has not come to light, nor has any proof that a liaison between Mick and the soon-to-be Mrs Paul McCartney went further than a wistful embrace beneath the stars at the conclusion of an evening out.

To an ultimately more pragmatic end, the Stones had also hooked up with the Ertegun brothers and a yapping disc jockey with the *nom de turntable* Murray The K. The brashest of them all, Murray had had the unmitigated audacity to style himself 'the fifth Beatle' and 'the sixth Rolling Stone'. Nevertheless, he had his uses; it was Murray, for example, who found the Stones the 'It's All Over Now' blueprint by The Valentinos, a soul act in which, incidentally, the Erteguns' Atlantic label were 'interested'.

That was jolly decent of Murray The K, but other of his countrymen expected more than a thank you for their kindnesses. With a mouth that spewed forth estimates at a moment's notice, Allen Klein, an accountant-manager from New Jersey, reminded The Kinks' Ray Davies of 'an archetypal villain in a film'.[17] Like many other US record-business folk, Klein had anticipated correctly further demand for UK talent and had crossed the ocean to stake claims in the musical diggings.

The fawning reverence of his employees was tempered by innumerable derogatory *bons mots* from former clients. Yet Allen's wheedling of a jaw-droppingly high advance for the Stones from Decca particularly impressed Paul McCartney, while to Ringo Starr he'd come across as 'a powerful man, and, also, no matter what anyone says, he's fair'.[18]

A prophecy that Klein would represent The Beatles before the Swinging '60s were out almost came as true as one other: that the Stones would be shaken from the grasp of Andrew Loog Oldham and Eric Easton by one of the fiercest lions in the US showbiz jungle.

7 Trouble In Mind

'It was the end of innocence, the end of the fun.'

– *Mick Jagger*[1]

Mick had been referred to disparagingly if indirectly when the headmaster read out a list of famous past pupils during Dartford Grammar's Founders' Day in 1965. Someone had also sawn off a section of an ink-welled desk lid mutilated with the initials 'MJ'.

Nevertheless, Jagger Major and his pop group were starting to be taken half-seriously. Broadsheets no longer put snooty inverted commas around their name, and swinging vicars would slip them into *Five To Ten*, an incongruous five-minute religious slot on the BBC Light Programme linking *Uncle Mac's Children's Favourites* and *Saturday Club*. From Moscow, the Soviet Ministry of Culture sent an emissary to a Stones concert in Warsaw. He returned so thoroughly horrified by what he had experienced that the Ministry made a firm decision not to let Western pop into Russia.

In Australia, where Mick made time to visit his maternal aunt and cousins, Richard Neville – founder of Sydney-based underground magazine *Oz* – wasn't so alarmist, writing that 'seeing Mick Jagger felt like seeing part of myself – as if the Stones and I, and all our mates, belonged to a secret tribe. The mode of the music was alchemical, Mick's strut signalling a burning impatience with the *ancien régime*.'[2]

Every vicinity across the continent contained an outfit that had reinvented itself as an *ersatz* British beat group. Sydney's Bee Gees, for instance, mutated from an updated Mills Brothers to quasi-

Beatles, while over in Melbourne a bunch of skifflers had found a Mick Jagger soundalike in future accountant Rod Turnbull and bowdlerised The Rolling Stones' name. What's more, The Spinning Wheels hired Roger Savage, the lately emigrated engineer of the Stones' first Decca session, and worked up a repertoire that was just as rife with – often the same – Diddley, Berry, Wolf, Waters and Reed favourites. Perhaps in some other universe, the Wheels are slaying 'em at the Hollywood Bowl while it's Jagger who's ended up amongst the ledgers when his time as the Medway Towns' 'answer' to Rod Turnbull has passed.

Back in Britain, the Stones had beaten off a too-real challenge by The Troggs, hailed on the *Andover Advertiser*'s very front page as 'The Greatest Group Since The Beatles!'[3] Could anyone not empathise with the local lads' pique when, before 'Wild Thing' fell from its high of Number Two, only the Stones' 'Paint It Black' stopped them from lording it on *Top Of The Pops*?

Jagger was sufficiently gripped by 'Wild Thing' to pop his head around the door to proffer advice during the taping of another Troggs smash, but Reg Presley, The Troggs' prime mover, articulated the view of a majority not in complete agreement with shifts in parameters of musical consciousness propagated by the likes of the Stones as the watershed year of 1967 loomed: 'Pop lately has got bogged down with cleverness. We have reverted to an elementary lyric and three elementary chords. "Wild Thing" was like a breath of fresh air to ordinary listeners. Pop music should be progressive, but it shouldn't wander too far ahead of the public.'[4]

Brian Jones had strummed a sitar on 'Paint It Black'; The Beatles would be jump-cutting from beat to 'Tomorrow Never Knows', the eerie omega to 1966's *Revolver*, with its tape collage and quotes from *The Tibetan Book Of The Dead*, while The Yardbirds were now far more than the 12-bar blues band they once were, even though they had near-enough the same guitar-bass-drums instrumental lineup as The Troggs.

Across the Atlantic, Bob Dylan had long stopped going on about war being wrong, fairer shares for all and so on, and was singing through his nostrils about myriad less wistful topics, revealing greater possibilities beyond protest and boy-meets-girl. Indeed, when *Oz* was launched in Britain, one edition featured a mind-boggling, word-for-word analysis of his 1966 12-minute album track 'Desolation Row' by an obsessive who, in order to prove one pet theory, had placed an ad in an *Oz*-like outlet in New York for a Dylan urine sample.

You'd have some trouble finding a corresponding Jagger-ologist, but as the wordsmith in his and Keith's partnership at that time he concurred with Phil May, his opposite number in The Pretty Things, that 'we couldn't sing about chain gangs because we'd never been on one. We were trying to get our language onto record, using R&B as a framework and later finding a new direction.'

The first Jagger–Richards A-side for the Stones, 1965's 'The Last Time', was in essence a modest affair with basic boy-girl rhyming couplets and a chorus borrowed from 'This May Be The Last Time', a traditional song popularised in 1953 by The Five Blind Boys Of Mississippi, a black gospel ensemble whose recorded works were purchasable in Dobell's.

Within a year, however, Mick had become as fluent and as individual a lyricist as Chuck Berry and Dylan. A track digging at a desperately trendy and finger-clicking publicist titled 'The Under-Assistant West Coast Promotion Man' had B-sided the US pressing of the epoch-making '(I Can't Get No) Satisfaction', a broader social comment that might have been a dissection of the Warhol-esque aesthetics of consumer culture or just Mick moaning about the vicissitudes of his travelling life. He'd never proffer a clue, 'because it's much more pleasurable for people to have their own interpretation of a song, novel, film or so on'.[5]

Thinking the worst, the host of *The Ed Sullivan Show* – North America's version of ITV's long-running variety showcase *Sunday Night At The London Palladium* – decreed the bleeping-out of *make* in the phrase 'trying to make some girl'.[6] Similarly, radio stations across the globe were unhappy about other bits, and English teachers were trying to repair the damage caused by the double negative in the song's very title.

'Satisfaction' would be the Stones' first US Number One and would be voted 1965's Best Single Of The Year in the *NME's* readers' poll in an age when the ordained strategy for keeping up a pop group's momentum was to rush-release as many 45s – usually four per fiscal year – as the traffic would allow.

Under pressure to capitalise on 'Satisfaction', Jagger and Richards came up with what, to Jim McCarty of The Yardbirds, was symptomatic of 'a bit of a lull artistically then, what with all those hits that were similar: "Satisfaction", "Get Off Of My Cloud", "19th Nervous Breakdown"…' Nevertheless, nowhere as disappointing a follow-up as The Beatles' 'Can't Buy Me Love' had been to 'I Want To Hold Your Hand' in 1964, 'Get Off Of My Cloud' tramped a well-trodden path to the top at home and lasted a fortnight against 'Satisfaction''s month there in the States. '19th Nervous Breakdown', however, stalled at Number Two in both charts after prompting one *Melody Maker* reviewer to comment, 'If this hadn't been recorded by the Stones, it wouldn't be a hit.'[7]

As an excitable schoolboy in the mid-1960s, I didn't agree, but maybe I was more snowblinded by the group's looks and corporate personality than *Melody Maker* and the Stones' very singer, who 'knew it wouldn't be as good, but so what? I used to write about 12 songs in two weeks on tour. It gives you lots of ideas. You're just totally into it. You get back from a show, have something to eat, a few beers, and just go to your room and write. At home, you don't want to do anything but read and things like that.'[8]

If simply a team player – albeit a vital one – in the studio, Jagger had been singled out, however unwillingly, as not only the Stones' central figure but also a separate entity. 'Is It Mick And The Stones Now?' asked a *Melody Maker* headline,[9] prompted perhaps by a televised 'Ready Steady Go Rave Mad Mod Ball' at Wembley's Empire Pool, when the five were introduced by Jimmy Savile as 'Jagger M and the Rolling Stones'.

Wait! That wasn't all. 'The main personality of the group is, of course, Mick Jagger,' confirmed Albert Hand in a *Teenbeat Monthly* editorial. 'He has managed to get away from the "group image". Especially on TV shows, one would imagine that the group was called Mick Jagger And The Stones by the sheer fact that the cameras are rarely off him!!!'[10]

Man of the moment Reg Presley's favourite vocalist, and the number one individual group member in a tabulation in *Record Mirror* – a publication that didn't trouble to hide its preference for the Stones over The Beatles – Mick had been present in spirit via The Manish Boys' singer renaming himself David *Bowie* (after the Wild West adventurer's idiosyncratic sidearm), as he'd heard that, apparently, 'jagger' in Old English meant 'knife'. Mick was there, too, in the Brooding Intensity and pooched-out lips of vocalists in The Game, Hamilton And The Movement, Dublin's Bluesville and others of multitudinous also-ran R&B outfits, who – as Jagger had with James Brown in TAMI – found it instructive to watch 1965's *NME* Pollwinners Concert 1965 for his 'faultless timing and knowing just where to put the emphasis in his phrasing'. The critic went on: 'The faster tempo of "Around And Around" saw Jagger going into his more violent movements, and he whirled around at one moment like a berserk windmill. Showing how important it is to give the audience something to watch as well as listen to, Mick's facial dramatics during "The Last Time" were an education.'[11]

Chris Jagger hadn't had to try as hard as Hamilton *et al* when, as 'Laurie Yarman', he won a Mick Jagger impersonation contest at Greenwich Town Hall in September 1964. However, unlike Paul McCartney's younger brother, Mike McGear, he wasn't using a stage name in order to stay accusations of his boarding his more illustrious sibling's bandwagon. On the contrary, he wrote an article about Mick 'as he really is' for the *NME*[12] and enquired into the feasibility of pursuing a pop career of his own with such a talismanic surname.

Meanwhile, Mick, a determined self-improver, was on the look-out for an opening in another sphere as soon as a gap appeared in the Stones' demanding schedule. Hardly a week was going by without some pop icon or other having a try at acting in a non-vacuous film. Dave Clark had been 'Steve' in *Catch Us If You Can*, John Lennon was to be 'Private Gripweed' in *How I Won The War*, and Paul Jones would keep biting his lip as a pop-star-turned-messiah in *Privilege*, with Jean Shrimpton in the female lead. After the Françoise Hardy idea foundered, it was reported that the Stones would make their first movie, *Rolling Stones*, about a group of drifters. Then there'd be talk of one about a conquest of Britain by wonderful-young-people, with Mick as 'Ernie', the main character.

While these proposals came and went, Jagger extended himself through the devil he knew when Andrew Oldham founded his own record label, Immediate, with The Small Faces, a flagship act with a backlog of hits for Decca and fronted by Steve Marriott. While Andrew wasn't able to sign the Stones *per se*, there was nothing to stop the band's members functioning in a behind-the-scenes capacity – just as Mick did as producer of Chris Farlowe, hitherto a blues and soul shouter from *norf* London, who'd meant next to nothing in the charts but was appreciated by other artists for a curdled baritone enhanced with strangled gasps and anguished roars that enabled him to take on items like 'In The Midnight Hour' and sound as thrilled as Wilson Pickett – the song's black originator – about the prospect of a tryst beneath the stars.

Farlowe's first Immediate 45, 1965's 'The Fool', was recorded under the supervision of Eric Burdon, but a more powerful ally was Jagger, who took charge of all Farlowe recordings for the next two years. 1966 began with 'Think' creating a stir. Next, another Jagger–Richards opus, 'Out Of Time', dragged Georgie Fame from Number One that summer. It didn't take long for the going to get rough again for Chris, but his triumph demonstrated that all he'd lacked was the right song – one that his producer thought worthy enough to graft his own lead vocal over the Farlowe backing track later, just in case it could be put to monetary use in the future. If neither a skinflint nor over-extravagant by nature, Jagger deplored waste.

A guitar-shaped swimming pool each could have been ordered by him and Richards on the strength of Farlowe's 'Out Of Time', and at least a diving board apiece for David Garrick's 'Lady Jane' and The Searchers' improvement on 'Take It Or Leave It', two other covers from *Aftermath*, the first Stones LP to consist entirely of compositions by Mick and Keith. The former praised Garrick to his face but wasn't especially complimentary in interview about his version of 'Lady Jane', which was as lushly orchestrated as the *Aftermath* arrangement wasn't. In doing so, Jagger hurt himself, as well as Garrick, financially, but he kept quiet about other syndications such as 'I Am Waiting' by The Quiet Five, Wayne Gibson's 'Under My Thumb' and 'Mother's Little Helper' from Gene Latter, who was accorded a modicum of press exposure by alleging that Mick had stolen his stage act.

Any artistic borrowing on disc only rounded off what were already strong songs that dwelt frequently on unexpected subjects. The aforementioned 'Mother's Little Helper' was an enduring scrutiny of the habit-forming tablets that hasten a frantic housewife's 'busy dying day', and riding roughshod over mitherings about its sexual arrogance, 'Under My Thumb' was still in the concert set 15 years later.

There'd be much to praise too about Jagger's libretto to the next collection, *Between The Buttons*. The *NME* noted 'shades of Dylan' pervading 'Who's Been Sleeping Here',[13] and the discerning Frank Zappa thought that the entire album was 'an important piece of social comment at the time'.[14] Yet he may have been nonplussed by a recording methodology that also appeared slap-dash to The Beach Boys' presiding genius, Brian Wilson, present at the session for track two, side one, 'My Obsession': 'There seemed to be a hell of a party in progress. Tables overflowed with booze, drugs and food. Girls were everywhere.'[15]

Nonetheless, at least the atmosphere wasn't sterile. It also drew from Mick a broad range of vocal expression, from bittersweetly sinister 'Back Street Girl' to his jocular valediction in 'Something Happened To Me Yesterday'. Who cares if he wasn't much of a singer, in a Scott Walker sense? At least Mick Jagger always sounded like Mick Jagger nowadays.

The euphonious Walker was magnanimous about him after a fashion when, following a vitriolic swipe at Tom Jones, he added, 'I'd sooner hear somebody who doesn't claim to be a great singer, like Mick Jagger.'[16] However, though it was partly through Mick's urging that The Walker Brothers had come to Britain in 1965 – rather than continue to kick their heels round Hollywood – Jagger and his entourage flicked lit cigarettes at Scott's table in a London club, having learned that 'Make It Easy On Yourself' by him and his unrelated relations had ended the reign of 'Satisfaction' at the top of the hit parade. Whether this was sour grapes or just good fun, a couple of bored journalists endeavoured to orchestrate a feud between Jagger and Walker by, for example, making something of the former greeting his girlfriend with a rendition of 'When My Shrimpboat Comes Home' – a parody of the Brothers' next smash, 'My Ship Is Coming In'.

It wouldn't be 'Mick and Chrissie' for much longer – although in as late as autumn 1966 she had been in the passenger seat when he crashed his midnight blue Aston D86 near his new flat in Harley House, a Marylebone mansion block. 'Stupid Girl' from *Aftermath* and 'Yesterday's Papers' from *Between The Buttons* were, purportedly, inspired by his fading love for Shrimpton, who by January was seeking comfort in the arms of Steve Marriott, who in turn was as jubilant as he could be that, in the meritocracy that was pop, one such as her could spare more than a second glance at 'a mere Small Face'.[17]

Ratifying the old rumour, Marianne Faithfull was now sharing Jagger's bed. If Chrissie had been upset, no one else was; Mick selected 'My Way Of Giving' – written by Marriott and fellow Small Face Ronnie Lane – as a Chris Farlowe A-side and John Dunbar was put in charge of the *son et lumière* for the Stones' spring tour of Europe.

The only public hint at disharmony came from an outsider, Jimi Hendrix, one of the most omnipotent of electric guitarists – and an overnight sensation – who'd arrived in London from New York in 1966 to form The Jimi Hendrix Experience, a platform for his showmanship as much as his riffs and solos, and his British drummer and bass player's quick-witted responses to them.

In common with Twinkle, Sandie Shaw and many other of UK pop's coltish *grandes dames*, Marianne perceived that, beneath it all, the exotic Jimi was an innocent abroad, a little-boy-lost type who needed mothering. This irritated Mick – especially as, before his very eyes, Hendrix started chatting up Marianne one night at the Speakeasy.

His knuckles may have whitened, but Jagger held onto his dignity and made light of it the next day. After all, what did a *parvenu* like Hendrix have on someone described in a condescending article in the *Evening Standard* as 'the most fashionably modish young man in London'? 'We are told he is the voice of today,' it continued, 'a today person, symptomatic of our society. Cecil Beaton paints him, says he is reminded of Nijinsky, of Renaissance angels; magazines report that he is a friend of Princess Margaret; gossip columns tell us what parties he failed to turn up at.'[18] Most of it was true, even if the Queen's sister was a fan of other pop stars, too, remarking to Spencer Davis, 'Your music has given me a great deal of pleasure.'[19]

Mick was also soon to be a neighbour of Commander David Birkin, a hero of Dunkirk; his wife, comedy actress Judy Campbell; and their daughter, Jane, listed as 'Blonde' in the closing credits of *Blow Up*, Antonioni's portrayal of Swinging London that had become a little antiquated by the time the flick was on general release late in 1966.

In the same cluster of Mewses, Places, Walks, Gardens and Rows in Chelsea – though elegant light-years away from ghastly Edith Grove – the Victorian painter James McNeill Whistler's old house along Cheyne Walk had been the setting for *Blow Up*'s orgy scene. On the same side of the road, Jagger set up home with Faithfull and her toddler, Nicholas, at number 48, built around 1710.

Searching for a country retreat too, Mick faced the problem of estate agents forcing up asking prices for those they presumed had wealth beyond calculation. However, via a go-between, Mick came across a bargain in 'Stargroves', a property in west Berkshire near the thatched cottage in the village of Aldworth that he'd later buy for Marianne's mother. The grander Stargroves, so he was assured, had been a field headquarters for the Roundheads during the Civil War.

It happened that Andrew Oldham's concomitant house-hunting had led him to a metropolitan mansion that really had been owned once by Oliver Cromwell's brother. That Oldham was no longer representing Marianne Faithfull had been symptomised in 1965 by him hedging his bets by producing both her and The Nashville Teens' singles of the same song, 'This Little Bird'. The Stones, too, were slipping through his fingers, thanks, seemingly, to a divide-and-conquer ploy by Allen Klein, appointed initially to oversee Andrew's business affairs.

More inclined to fire than hire, Klein had convinced Oldham that too much capital was being wasted on too many Billy Bunters whose postal orders never arrived, and that Eric Easton's face no longer fitted. However, Eric had been a loyal and essentially honest servant, as well as trustful, and it wasn't surprising that an attempt to buy out the man who'd shared the Stones' fortunes since 1963 was thwarted, and a shower of writs ensued. If tiring of ideas that were more intriguing conceptually than in ill-conceived practice, Oldham would cling on longer, until the day in 1968 when he rang Jagger from a telephone booth to wish him a good rest of his life.

In January 1967, Andrew had had to calm friction when the Stones had agreed to star on *Sunday Night At The London Palladium*, with its endless centuries of stand-up comics, crooners, The Tiller Girls dance-troupe and the famed 'Beat The Clock' interlude. The time-honoured finale always had all the performers lined up on the rim of the theatre's revolving stage. Whenever members of a pop group hove into view, the pit orchestra's 'Startime' play-out would be swamped by screams that would ebb abruptly as they were carried off to the back, to be replaced by an almost palpable wave of goodwill washing over some national treasure of a comedian like Max Bygraves or Frankie Howerd; less so for the second-string Ted Rogers or Terry Scott.

On this occasion, however, there was a snag when the Stones' turn came. Mick and, by implication, the other four refused to join the farewell roundabout, arguing that, family audience or not, he wasn't prepared to compromise the group's anti-everything stance. Perhaps he was still peeved about the likes of Rogers taking the mick, and Bygraves poking fun with the aid of an overhead projector on the same programme a few months earlier. Alternatively, if he'd even watched these jokers, Jagger might have laughed along with everybody else, just as he might have grinned askance when, on another *Palladium* show, cabaret singer Margo Henderson belted out the traditional gospel song, 'Down By The Riverside', updated to include a reference to 'the good old Rolling Stones'.

Predictable howls of affronted derision from the 'straight' press over the group's behaviour on *Sunday Night At The London Palladium* was still resonating during the next edition's rotating curtain call, when Peter Cook and Dudley Moore stood waving next to their cardboard effigies of the Stones.

The satirical pair had maximised their small-screen popularity by taking potshots at the Top 50, most recently with the spoof 'LS Bumble Bee', a single that was indicative of a general knowledge, if not use, of LSD, which had been part of the anything-goes spirit of Swinging London for about a year before it was outlawed for recreational purposes in 1966. The drug had already launched Brian Jones and Keith Richards on a fantastic voyage that was to carry them further from olde-tyme beat music than anyone who'd bought 'Come On' could have foreseen.

By comparison, Mick – as befitted the son of a physical fitness expert – had had little to do with narcotics of any description. He'd hesitated before sampling marijuana for the first time, purportedly, in a cigarette rolled by Paul McCartney at the Beatle's house in St John's Wood. Nevertheless, once Jagger got around to LSD, too, he was loud in its defence as a chemical handmaiden to self-discovery: 'You see everything aglow. You see yourself beautiful and ugly, and other people as if for the first time. You should take it in the country, surrounded by all those flowers. You'd have no bad effects. It's only people who hate themselves that suffer.'[21]

In so doing, Jagger was not only gilding his national notoriety but also identifying with a spreading hippy subculture disturbing enough to warrant a celebrity-freighted campaign to curtail it. At a public meeting, Frankie Vaughan – once the Stones to Dickie Valentine's Beatles – declared that 'hippies are leeches on society',[22] spurning a flower proffered by one such leech in the audience.

Vaughan's counter-revolution would gather pace with his new single, 1967's 'There Must Be A Way' – along with those by Tom Jones, Engelbert Humperdinck and Cliff Richard – nestling awkwardly in the autumn Top 20 amongst entries from the psychedelic likes of The Small Faces, Jimi Hendrix, Traffic, The Move – and The Rolling Stones, whose 'We Love You' was a mock-placatory riposte to an ugly episode during which the 'establishment' had all but won a decisive victory.

8 Worried Life Blues

'I met a fellow who'd been at school with Mick and I. He'd become a cop in Chelsea, and he said, "I saw Jagger the other day, and I was thinking of busting him just for the hell of it."'

– Dick Taylor

Apart from the preponderance of 'decent music' in the charts, the us-and-them situation had intensified, initially with laughable minor attritions such as the arrest of a youth for blowing bubbles – a 'breach of the peace' – in Trafalgar Square. Well, he had long hair, hadn't he? It was flattery of a sort if you looked hippyish enough to be stopped and searched for drugs. Overloaded vans transporting bands and equipment were pulled over by bored squad cars, who'd prise off speaker-cabinet covers in their search for hidden substances.

Why were the screws tightening all of a sudden? 'The hippy revolution was beginning to make an impact,' recalled Caroline Coon, a London student whose boyfriend was serving time then for possession of marijuana, 'and causing the establishment to recoil in horror. Young people were literally disappearing off the streets. Nobody knew where they'd gone. Doors were being kicked down at two o'clock in the morning and the police would barge in.'[1]

It wasn't, therefore, just the ineffectual Alf Garnetts who held that it was their bounden duty to go beyond merely bemoaning what certain Sunday newspapers saw as the encroaching godlessness of the age, even if its currency of narcotics and interrelated promiscuity wasn't especially valid outside London and the bigger cities. Alternatively, it was understandable that a lot of 'them' were eating their hearts out, either because their dreary husbands were the only men they'd ever slept with or because their teenage years had been blighted by national service; being compelled by the government to endure hair being planed halfway up the side of the skull; a kitting-out with an ill-fitting, dung-coloured uniform; and getting bawled at from dawn till dusk.

If there was a war on, you or the bloke marching next to you might have finished it with an empty sleeve, shell-shocked or blinded – and today you heard some little twerp answering back when his poor old mother told him to get off to the barber's for a four-penny all-off! What sort of world was it when you switched on the television and that Mick Jagger flashed into the living room, hair all over his surly, lippy mug, poncing about in his flowery tat and caterwauling that he couldn't get no satisfaction unless he and some tart spent the night together? That was if you could make out the words, which you couldn't.

Jagger was therefore among 'their' most wanted outlaws, even if his lookalikes were common enough now in the sticks as well as the big cities. Yet he began as a mere bystander, almost in the wings, when the curtains rose on the most overt act in a drama hitherto exceptional only for a *divertissement* in which two *News Of The World* witch-hunters, mistaking Brian Jones for Mick, had banged out a report assuring readers, several months after the fact, that he had quite openly swallowed some amphetamine tablets and invited them back to his flat to smoke some hashish – or was it LSD?

When an outraged Jagger served a libel suit, the editor carpeted the journalists responsible and plotted a damage-limitation scheme whereby the truth – or at least *a* truth – could be re-timed. By prodding various nerves, he discovered that Jagger and Marianne Faithfull were to spend a weekend during 1967's mild February at 'Redlands', Keith Richards' moated grange in the peninsula banked by Hayling Island and Chichester. It was a matter of a couple of telephone calls to West Sussex Regional Police Headquarters to arrange for the place to be invaded on the Sunday evening.

Sure enough, the officers found enough drugs on the premises to justify the arrest of Richards and – to *The News Of The World*'s relief – a subdued Jagger, even if it had to be trumped up from four pep pills that – so it was pointed out in court four months later – were available over the counter across the Channel, and that his doctor had permitted him to retain them to combat pressure of work. The bench overruled this defence; less than ten minutes later, the jury – in which folklore was to include Terry Scott – returned a 'guilty' verdict, and two days later an intrinsically law-abiding 23-year-old who only wanted to get to the dock quietly was steered from his cell in unnecessary handcuffs and, amid extravagant rejoicing and lamentation, sent down for three months.

He managed not to faint, but the famous mouth was almost comical in its gaping shock, and tears weren't far away as he was hustled out of the Chichester courtroom and off to Brixton Prison, more convenient than it might have been for visits from his parents, who were still in Wilmington and still 'unhappy with what I do',[2] as he'd admit long after this particular storm had passed. Eva and Joe would, however, not be obliged to enter the institution's high and forbidding walls, as their Mike was granted bail after not quite two days behind bars.

In the interim, the BBC had wrung its hands over whether or not to pan away from Jagger when that Thursday's *Top Of The Pops* broadcast the pre-recorded performance of The Beatles' flower-power anthem 'All You Need Is Love', in which the convict had been among the turnout of illustrious friends assisting on the *omnes fortissimo* hooklines. That same week, a poster with Mick's image and the paraphrased caption 'LET HE WHO IS WITHOUT SIN JAIL THE FIRST STONE' was in hippy shops; protest marches along Fleet Street were broken up with the aid of police Alsatians, and a last-minute insert in the latest edition of *Oz* disclosed the home address of *The News Of The World*'s editor, along with a sly caution that 'It would be inadvisable for our readers to mail him cannabis resin and then tip off the police in an effort to have him busted.'[3]

Its own kind turned on *The News Of The World*, too. The party line at both *The Sun* and the *Daily Sketch* was that the incarceration was 'too likely to make a martyr of this wretched young man',[4] while the *Sunday Express* weighed in with its opinion that it was 'monstrously out of proportion to the offence'.[5]

On the evening after his sentence was commuted to a conditional discharge and the judge reminded him of his 'grave responsibilities', Jagger was trotted out before ITV cameras to debate the repercussions of his conduct since he'd first touched the brittle fabric of fame, with two high-ranking priests, a former Home Secretary and the writer of a fiercely sympathetic editorial in *The Times*. Belying both his trembling mind and the assumptions by many viewers that he was some sort of anomalous retard, the former LSE undergraduate who was now the kingdom's most reviled and worshipped celebrity gave an intelligent and gently spoken account of himself, not exactly repudiating the taking of illegal drugs, but arguing with calm sense that he wasn't the one who'd made an issue of it in the first place. As a mere pop singer, he'd been unqualified to do so in any case, unconsciously agreeing with the *Daily Express*'s James MacMillan, who was then sharpening his quill to express indignant wonder that such a discussion had ever wasted television time.

Though the *Express* had also published a cartoon in which a John Bull-like figure voices disgust that 'Mick Jagger, Rolling Stone' had become 'Mick Jagger, Saint!',[6] the heavy-handed endeavour to punish Mick Jagger for being Mick Jagger backfired further when his case – following so soon after that of her boyfriend – escalated Caroline Coon's foundation of Release, 'the first youth organisation that was really an alternative social service run by young people for young people', she said with quiet pride. 'I felt people needed to know what to do when they were arrested, that you didn't have to be pressured into a confession. You didn't have to make a statement before you've seen a solicitor. What the police claim to be illegal drugs must be confirmed by analysis. You are legally entitled to a telephone call, etc. One of the first practical things we did at Release was put out a know-your-rights Bust Card. We had thousands printed to distribute free.'[1]

Finally, the conclusion to the best-known drugs trial in pop 'gave the Stones this image of being like a real bunch of dope fiends',[7] sniggered Jagger.

A more profound upset of the group's equilibrium, however, was rooted in Keith stealing Anita Pallenberg from Brian. Near-unbearable tension, onstage and off, was to be exacerbated further by the first stirrings of a real-life enactment of that soap-opera cliché whereby the greater the antagonism between two characters, the greater the likelihood that they will become lovers. 'Mick really tried to put me down,' grimaced Anita, 'but there was no way that this crude guy was going to do a number on me. I found out that, if you stand up to Mick, he crumbles.'[8]

Carnal self-interest and other complications of personal alliances informed the recording of *Their Satanic Majesties Request*, the first Stones album without Andrew Oldham in charge. Now that Sir had left the classroom, the children started doing what they liked. 'It was a really fun moment,' agreed Mick, 'and there were some good songs on it. There's a lot of rubbish, too; just too much time on our hands, too many drugs, no producer to tell us, "Enough!" Anyone let loose in the studio will produce stuff like that. It's like believing everything you do is great and not having any editing, and Andrew had gone by that point. The reason he left was because he thought we weren't concentrating and that we were being childish.'[9]

I'm one of those heretics who thinks that *Satanic Majesties* might be one of the Stones' finest albums, though I never went as far as to spin it in the dark, at the wrong speeds and often enough to comprehend veiled but oracular messages. Nevertheless, I picked up on trifles such as a muffled 'Where's that joint?' (which might have been 'Where's that johnny?') from Mick over the introit to the reprise of 'Sing This Song Altogether'. The album remains tied very much to pop's fleeting 'classical' period, straddling as it does genres as otherwise irreconcilable as music hall and John Cage-esque electronic collage and depending on a fragmentary concept – just like The Beatles' *Sgt Pepper's Lonely Hearts Club Band*, which is replete with similarly elaborate and expensive packaging and awash with real and imagined symbolism.[10]

Yet, paralleling The Pretty Things' *SF Sorrow* – unquestionably the first rock opera (though technically a song cycle) – the Stones' absorption of psychedelic trendiness and their late hours of console twiddling didn't smother entirely the raw blues-wailing edge of old, as it had when, say, Steve Winwood from The Spencer Davis Group managed a transition via his new outfit, Traffic, to pixified 'Hole In My Shoe'. However, the Stones were to prove just as capable of nursery-rhyme tweeness with 'Dandelion' on the other side of the 'We Love You' single. The only trick they missed was a kiddie chorus.

Other diverse signs of the times were the sitar *obbligato* – rather than a busking saxophone – gnawing at Jagger's production of the jazz standard 'Moanin'' as Chris Farlowe's latest 45 – and Mick and Marianne cramming into the same compartment as The Beatles and the Maharishi Mahesh Yogi during 1967's August Bank Holiday on what has been dubbed the 'Mystical Express': an odyssey from Euston to north Wales, where the guru was to lead an initiation course in transcendental meditation that lasted nearly a fortnight and involved talks about karma, the transmigration of souls and the world of illusion. Not sure whether the Maharishi was a charlatan or a seer, Jagger, waylaid by a bellowed question from the crush of fans and media at the station, had dismissed the outing straightaway as 'more like a circus than the beginning of an original event'.[11]

For one who'd lived in more of a world of illusion than most since 1963, it was perhaps too much of an adventure. Hard cash had become as unnecessary to Mick and The Beatles as eyesight to a monkfish, and they were at a loss when handed the bill after a meal in a Bangor restaurant. George Harrison was the first to realise why the waiters kept hovering around the table, and it was he, too, who settled the matter with a roll of banknotes he chanced to have – as you do – in the hollow sole of his shoe.

Neither this incident nor the hard mattresses in the student accommodation on the University of Bangor campus were as disconcerting as the press conference that the Maharishi's PR agent had set up in the main hall. It was here that most trailing newshounds appeared to treat flippantly the preoccupation with meditation demonstrated by those whom one scribe's notepad had listed as 'John Lennon, Paul, George, Ringo and *Jagger*' –whose stay was curtailed after two days by the sudden death of Brian Epstein in a Swinging London that was now at the forefront of the inevitable commercialisation of flower-power.

The West End musical *du jour* then was *Hair*, imported from New York and destined to run for 11 years. While the fundamental plot centred on a youth eligible for induction into the US Army, it also delved into aspects of hippy culture, with the tabloids making much of the murkily lit nakedness that closed the first half, as well as the extremity of improvisation and audience participation. Fortunately, *Hair* was blessed with memorable songs that were eventually to infiltrate the realms of jazz and Las Vegas cabaret. More immediate, however, were a rash of cover versions, such as 'Aquarius' by both Paul Jones and, in German, Spencer Davis. From the cast, Sonja Kristina, Paul Nicholas and Alex Harvey were all to crack the domestic charts, one way or another, and so – just – was Marsha Hunt, a singing actress who was to have a pronounced bearing on Mick Jagger's life.

Of mixed race but raised in Pennsylvania, Marsha had been a member of Free At Last, a blues trio led by Alexis Korner. Unfinanced, the group struggled to survive from its earliest rehearsals in a Soho basement, prior to Hunt's membership of

Long John Baldry's Bluesology and then The Ferris Wheel, who specialised in competent work-outs of US soul. By contrast, she also rehearsed with The Soft Machine, a progressive outfit featuring her future husband, Mike Ratledge, on keyboards. At the time, however, she was living with John Mayall, whose albums with his Blues Breakers sold steadily if unremarkably.

Dissatisfied with her artistic progress, Marsha contemplated her next move during a six-month break, when she considered *au pairing* and even resuming her poetry studies at the University of California. There were also attempts at learning the bass guitar – borrowed from Fleetwood Mac's John McVie – as an avenue for songwriting. Then someone mentioned that auditions were being held at the Shaftesbury Theatre for *Hair*.

When the show opened, the first face you were drawn to was Marsha's, mainly for her wide shock of fuzzy black hair. *Disc & Music Echo* thought so, too, and featured a full-colour double-page head-and-shoulders portrait one week. She was also commensurate with Mick Jagger's apparent penchant for 'girls with long dark hair, who are small and gay. She must be interesting and interested in me. She must be fully aware of the pop scene.'[12] These words – perhaps calculated to needle Marianne – appeared in an edition of *Boyfriend*, proving that the Stones weren't so far above the adoration of schoolgirls that they didn't have recent photographs available on request for such a publication, along with *Rave!*, *Fabulous 208 et al.*

The latter gazette seemed to be reflecting teenage interest in rugged cowboy types like Doug McClure in *The Virginian* on BBC1 as much as, say, pretty Peter Frampton of The Herd, the soon-to-cease *Rave!*'s 'Face Of '68'. In more serious-minded journals pitched at youth, there was a divide too – between vulgar 'pop' and 'rock', which only the finest minds could grasp. The latter genre was now being shepherded away from psychedelic contrivance by such as Bob Dylan, with his austere, understated and lyrically direct *John Wesley Harding* [*sic*], and by a wave of good-time blues outfits like Canned Heat from Los Angeles, who balanced humour and scholarly application, much of it emanating from the differing natures of its mainstays: corpulent, jocose ex-supermarket charge hand Bob 'Bear' Hite and intense Al 'Blind Owl' Wilson, who held a master's degree.

The likes of Dylan and Canned Heat also convinced fans that singles were marginal to a main body of work on albums, while The Beatles spared themselves from having to be 'real' musicians in front of non-screaming rock customers by retiring to the studio. So, for different reasons, did Scott Walker – now parted from his Brothers and established as both principal interpreter for Belgian *chansonnier* Jacques Brel and as an intriguing composer in his own right – and The Dave Clark Five, whose leader was taking acting lessons.

Celluloid renown was to prove elusive for Dave, but, while she was not as easily hoisting her records into the charts, Marianne Faithfull[13] was making a fair fist of Shakespeare and Chekhov on the stage and had been approached by director Pierre Koralnik to be a wayward foreign foil to the refined 'Anna' for a musical of the same name composed by Serge Gainsbourg, slated to be the first colour programme on France's new second nationally networked channel.[14]

There were also prominent parts in feature films, such as Michael Winner's *I'll Never Forget Whatshisname* – in which Faithfull was the first to utter the F-word in a mainstream movie – and Roger Vadim's semi-pornographic *Girl On A Motorcycle*,[15] which prompted a reviling in the US Christian publication *Modern Dating* for 'tyrannising receptive minds with illicit sex, rebellion against parents, rebellion against society, crime, delinquency and romance'[16], and speculation by the *NME*'s Alley Cat tittle-tattler about what Mick thought of his paramour's love scenes with French heart-throb Alain Delon.

Doggedly, Jagger sat through *Girl On A Motorcycle*, and had been there at every one of 1967's spring evenings when Marianne had trod the boards in *Three Sisters* at the Chichester Festival, sending her a potted orange tree instead of a first-night bouquet of flowers.

These days, it was just Mick, rather than the Stones *en bloc*, who was being courted by theatre and movie moguls, either on the lookout for new talent or driven by cynical expediency, believing that the words 'Mick Jagger' in the credits would guarantee attention. In autumn 1968, he not so much dipped a toe as plunged head-first into a film, *Performance*, which had a screenplay by Donald Cammell, a leading light of the bohemian post-Second World War 'Chelsea Set' of jazzers, painters, debutantes, ex-public schoolboys, the more glamorous criminals – and, by the mid-1960s, the most *outré* pop musicians. Cammell was also a godson of Satanist wizard Aleister Crowley (who was included in the front-cover montage of *Sgt Pepper*).

If ostensibly a gangster flick, Cammell's script delved into existentialism and identity crises, notably when outlines dissolved between Jagger's 'Turner', a pop recluse, and 'Chas', a square but bisexual hitman (played by James Fox as a departure from his usual upper-class parts) fleeing from both rough justice and the police to Turner's 'right piss-hole' of 'long hairs, beatniks, druggers, free love... You couldn't find a better little hidey-hole.'[17]

When the film was finally on general release, you'd find, too, one of Mick Jagger's most powerful artistic statements. Any argument that his success with the Stones created the opportunity to do so – or that years of acting out his songs on the boards had taught him 'to other be' more effectively than most – is irrelevant. I'm taking no great critical risks here, but, though drawing from the recesses of his own character and personal history, Jagger in *Performance* was to blow away like dust the efforts of Dave Clark, Paul Jones, John Lennon and nearly every other British pop star of his vintage who ever had a go at 'proper' film acting.

9 The Devil's Shoestring

'Turner is supposed to be a great writer, like Dylan, but he's completely immersed in himself. He's a horrible person, really.'

– Mick Jagger[1]

Because *Performance* wasn't a breezy crime caper set in the Swinging London of *Blow Up*, Warner Brothers, its investors, did not accept the director's cut of the X-certificate film without comment. The violence was too sickening and the sex too weird and graphic. It was to be postponed indefinitely, and the re-editing – in which a scene of Jagger and Fox kissing had to be scissored, regardless – was to be subjected to the closest scrutiny, with extra-special attention paid to the troilism involving Jagger and the two female leads, Michele Breton and Anita Pallenberg, with whom Donald Cammell had been friendly before *Performance* was so much as a twinkle in his eye.

Passionate social adversaries as they were, there had been moments as long and as dangerous between Anita and Mick as those between Anita and Keith prior to her finishing with Brian. Derisive comments were a sublimation of a physical attraction that had been unleased in the huge bed on set where they were required to simulate sexual congress. To the crew projecting lenses beneath the sheets, there was more than enough realism in the pair's 'method acting', and certainly enough to persuade Marianne Faithfull – who miscarried days after filming was completed – that Jagger and Pallenberg had actually screwed. Richards was as discountenanced when he too watched what *Time*'s reviewer would brand 'the most disgusting, the most completely worthless film I have ever seen'.[2] Traumatised by what he'd witnessed both on and off camera, James Fox became an evangelical Christian, while Michele Breton, allegedly, never performed professionally again.

Yet there was no doubt that Mick Jagger had proved himself as natural a screen actor as Elvis Presley, who'd shone from the mire of *Paradise Hawaiian Style*, *Girl Happy* and the rest of the streamlined Hollywood vanities that had occupied him for most of the decade. Moreover, when permitted a say in the evolution of the plot, Jagger had made shrewd suggestions about lighting, wardrobe and pacing as he gathered the beginnings of a working knowledge of film production. For instance, when required to step backwards a couple of yards in a confined space, he introduced the hitherto untried idea of pushing drawing pins into the floorboards so that the touch of his bare feet on them would guide him into the preordained position for the next shot.

The fact that his abilities had testified to virtues other than mere publicity value meant that there was pressure to agree to more film assignments, forcing some unwise decisions. 'I made dumb movies and turned down the ones I should have done,'[3] he would admit – and, certainly, he never got around to a flick halfway as appealing as *Performance*. At one point, he reportedly approved a treatment by Nigel Gordon – an associate of The Pink Floyd – of the quest for the Holy Grail, with Marianne earmarked to be the Lady of Shallot. Jagger also dithered over something called *The Maxigasm* and a screen adaptation of Dennis Wheatley's *Lucifer Rising*. Holding the decision at arm's length, he suggested his brother instead to the latter's director – and Crowley disciple – Kenneth Anger, knowing full well that Chris was then backpacking in India for much of a gap year between Dartford Grammar and university.

After *Lucifer Rising* fizzled out, a pen was thrust into Mick's hand to sign a contract that was to lumber him with the title role in an updating of *Ned Kelly And His Gang*, a silent bio-pic that had appeared less than three decades after bushranger Kelly – romanticised as a sort of digger Robin Hood – had been hanged in Melbourne in 1880. Room was found for Marianne to play Kelly's 'Maid Marian'.

Even so, the trail hadn't yet gone cold on a silver-screen project for all the Stones. Every unforgiving minute of 'two very good nights', estimated Mick,[1] spent working on 'Sympathy For The Devil' – opening track of a new LP, *Beggars Banquet* – was documented by Jean-Luc Godard, whose ex-wife, Anna Karina, had been 'Anna' in Serge Gainsbourg's musical of the same name. One of the more challenging figures of French cinema, Godard 'understands music better than any director, alive or dead', reckoned Mike Figgis, an acquaintance of Charlie Watts and then an aspiring film-maker himself.[4]

Jean-Luc was so captivated by the new Jagger–Richards song that he had abandoned the working title, *One Plus One*, for *Sympathy For The Devil* by the time the picture was shown at the London Film Festival in November 1968. A slow-moving 99 minutes, it had been intended to contrast construction (the Stones creating 'Sympathy For The Devil') and destruction (a girl's suicide when deserted by her lover), but was now remodelled with no linking narrative between footage from the recording sessions, Black Power militants in a Battersea car dump, a television interview with some woman ('Eve Democracy') in a forest, her spraying graffiti all over London, and this geezer reading excerpts from *Mein Kampf* in a bookshop selling pornography. It was an Art Statement, like, and also topical enough to look dated now.

'Revolution is this year's flower power'[5] – so Frank Zappa had summed up 1968. There was so much to spark off the general uprising, so many common denominators: the Soviet rape of Czechoslovakia; the assassinations of Martin Luther King and Robert Kennedy; a compounding of feminism; the continued slaughter and starvation caused by Mao Tse Tung's cultural purge; Ireland, bloody Ireland – and, of course, Vietnam, where a

Lieutenant William Calley had just massacred the women and children of an entire village. Thus kaftans were mothballed as their former wearers followed the crowd to genuinely violent demonstrations, riots, student sit-ins and disruptions of beauty pageants. Girls lost their marbles over Daniel Cohn-Bendit – 'Danny The Red' – organiser of the 'situationist' New Left *événements* in France, but not as much as they did over the late Cuban *guerrillero* Che Guevara.

Interviewed at Cheyne Walk by Richard Branson, editor of the leftish *Student* magazine, Jagger, while seeming to be all for pacifism, dissident popular opinion and Cohn-Bendit's *soixante-huitards*, made no doctrinal statement. Yes, he'd been visible on a traffic island on the periphery of the militant protesters outside the US Embassy in London. Furthermore, 'Street Fighting Man' – another *Beggars Banquet* opus, and a US single – had been born of both this and Danny The Red's overseas activities that May, but Jagger qualified the song's sentiments with 'It's stupid to think you can start a revolution with a record. I wish you could.'[6]

Nevertheless, while not as pointed a rallying cry as, say, The Kinks' 'Every Mother's Son' – which peaceniks sang *en masse* outside the White House during the Vietnam moratorium – 'Street Fighting Man' acquired million-selling outsider chic when banned by both the BBC and – in the light of alarmist talk about the forthcoming 1968 National Democratic Convention – various radio stations in Chicago, where Mayor Daley had ordered police to 'shoot to kill' marching trouble-makers.

While Jagger would be criticised by agit-prop extremists for not inciting the half-million at the Stones' celebrated free concert in Hyde Park to take over London, he would volunteer financial aid when the saga of the notorious 'Schoolkids' edition of *Oz* climaxed at the Old Bailey, and had actually sunk hard cash into and procured premises for the British operation of San Francisco's groovily subversive *Rolling Stone*, which until then had not been readily available outside the States. He settled down eagerly to his duties as newspaper proprietor, hoping that the UK publication was to be developed separately from its Californian template.

This entrepreneurial sideshow, however, was to be thrust aside as the Stones' business dealings became more and more rife with discord. It was a mixed blessing that Allen Klein had been around less of late, having been hired to straighten out The Beatles' sprawling Apple empire, a venture that had taken mere weeks to snowball into chaos. Now something of a pop personality in his own right – as Andrew Loog Oldham and Brian Epstein had been – Klein was to demonstrate his worth via a re-negotiation of a royalty rate that amassed millions for The Beatles – albeit a Beatles soon to disband – within months.

Yet, once so pleased with Allen's bellicose interventions on the Stones' behalf, Jagger had taken the time to call at Apple to dissuade John, George, Ringo and Paul from signing with someone he couldn't yet accuse outright of shifty manoeuvres and illicit transfer of cash into his own account. Klein, however, had arrived before him, and was spieling in top gear.

As no one else was prepared to do so, Mick next applied skills learned at the LSE to studying the Stones' company ledgers, and taking measures to curb what he perceived as embezzlements and fiddles. Whenever possible, he also stuck to conventional office hours in the group's new headquarters on a single floor of a town house just off Piccadilly.

He was a fair-minded if fastidious boss, but his staff could not imagine him after work relaxing over an after-dinner crossword or watching *Panorama* while sipping a cup of cocoa. Mr Jagger had, after all, projected himself as the *comme il faut* but fiendish figure on the fringe of events detailed in 'Sympathy For The Devil', but sufficiently well placed to cause a stir for private amusement, whether a face in the crowd at Golgotha for the Crucifixion, in conference with Hitler 'when the Blitzkrieg raged and the bodies stank', or behind the steering wheel of JFK's limousine at Dallas. When the President's younger brother died at the trigger-jerk of another maniac in June 1968, the infallibly pragmatic Jagger had made the line 'I shouted out, "Who killed John Kennedy!"' plural (ie 'Who killed the Kennedys?').

Lucifer had been present in spirit too in *Their Satanic Majesties Request*. Since then, Mick had appeared on the cover of *The Process*, mouthpiece of the Church Of The Final Judgement and a magazine that, like *Oz*, was going the rounds of sixth-form common rooms. However, Marianne – who had articulated her perspective in an issue dedicated to 'Death' – regarded her more distant inamorata as 'far too sensible and normal ever to have become seriously involved in black magic. "Sympathy For The Devil" was pure *papier-mâché* Satanism.'[7]

The craze for theatrical diabolism was traceable in Britain to Screaming Lord Sutch, carried onto the boards in a coffin. It picked up speed when The Crazy World Of Arthur Brown – the toast of London's psychedelic dungeons – went public with 1967's 'Devil's Grip' before going for the jugular with chart-topping 'Fire!', featuring Arthur as 'god of hellfire' set to 'destroy all you've done'. Next up were outfits like Black Sabbath, with their inverted crosses and similar Satanic fetishist gear, and Black Widow, whose onstage 'sacrifice' of a naked woman during an audience-participation number, 'Come To The Sabbat', ensured healthy attendances at their engagements on the college circuit. Perusing *Melody Maker* as a stockbroker would the *Financial Times*, Mick would remark, 'There's a big following for these hocus-pocus bands, so obviously the subject has a vast commercial potential.'[8]

Rock 'n' roll revival was in the air too. As a company director, it was incumbent upon Jagger to supply sturdy goods, and market research intimated that it might be viable to turf a raw three-chord bedrock with *Satanic Majesties*-type lyricism.

The Stones' first domestic chart-topper since 'Paint It Black' ages ago in 1966, 'Jumpin' Jack Flash' had been previewed a fortnight before its release when a rumour swept music lovers at May 1968's otherwise routine *New Musical Express* Poll Winners' concert at

Wembley's Empire Pool that an attraction more famous than the rest of the bill put together was to make a surprise appearance. Some smart alec, while not wanting to build anyone's hopes up, said he'd just noticed three of The Downliners Sect backstage, and that Frankie Vaughan was stuck in a traffic jam on the North Circular. With credulity stretched to the limit, some were weeping with anticipation when Jimmy Savile announced The Rolling Stones. The place exploded, not a note was heard of 'Jumpin' Jack Flash' and 'Satisfaction', and Mick Jagger's shoe sailed into the crowd with one particularly energetic Tiller Girl-esque goose step.

On a nationwide scale, the Stones' comeback – the proverbial 'something to tell your grandchildren about' – eclipsed totally Chris Jagger's return from the East with a North American girlfriend. Among temporary jobs that he took to keep the wolf from the door before he started university was decorating Marsha Hunt's flat, and it would be through her recommendation that he'd be snapped up for a production of *Hair* in Israel.

Marsha herself was about to harry the lower half of the Top 50 with 'Walk On Gilded Splinters', an eerie blending of psychedelia and Creole chants. With a matching visual presentation, *Top Of The Pops* viewers were to be regaled by Marsha's voodoo choreography, which exposed sufficient cleavage to jam the BBC switchboard – and Mick enjoyed the knowledge that, unlike the millions of other men under her flickering spell that evening, he'd actually had sex with her.

After the loss of the baby, there'd been less lust in Mick for Marianne, yet he was still wearily astonished at how much his pride smarted when she made eyes at his friends and associates, and filled him with ugly suspicions. He reciprocated with affairs, of which the most costly in the long run would be with Marsha.

Both Mick and Marianne were not yet beyond dropping urbane public masks and feigned aloofness at home for abrupt reconciliations and making grand gestures of moral and material generosity, if not to rekindle the fire of their courtship then to remind each other what it had been like. He observed covertly that the strain of life at Cheyne Walk was draining her of her vivacity – and her beauty – but for now there remained an affection that manifested itself in laughter at each other's fantasies, shared recollections, impulsive embraces and the harmless verbal reviling of each other the way longtime intimates do.

For several months, too, they would be bound by a specific common ordeal. Despite the ultimate outcome of Jagger's arrest at Redlands, the police weren't finished with the Stones and their sort. Even The Beatles – national treasures or not – weren't above the law any more, as testified by recent busts of Lennon and Harrison. There were, however, hints of extra-legal procedures. 'Hundreds of young people came to Release with shocking stories of police corruption,' averred Caroline Coon. 'Many people, even George Harrison, were ringing up and saying truthfully, "I was planted."'[9]

According to files released by the Director of Public Prosecutions 35 years later, Mick Jagger stated that it had happened to him, too. A stake-out of 48 Cheyne Walk by plain-clothes officers under the direction of Detective Sergeant Robin Constable, head of the Chelsea Narcotics Squad, had ended just before 8 pm on 28 May 1969 with the apprehension of Jagger as he left the house, intending to drive to a recording session. When a search warrant was produced, it was later claimed that the defendant yelled in the direction of an open basement window, 'Marianne, don't open the door! It's the police! They're after the weed!'

As a slang expression, 'weed' was as outmoded in 1969 as 'too much' had been in the 1950s after young clergymen started slipping it into conversations with youth clubbers. Furthermore, Faithfull later maintained, 'I never heard anyone shout, but I saw someone's hand over Mick's mouth. I assumed that he was being attacked by thugs and ran from the kitchen upstairs to the front door, which I opened. At this, Mick shouted, "Shut the door, you silly twit! It's the police!"'

Years later, Constable would be cleared of corruption at a hearing chaired by his Scotland Yard superiors, but Jagger felt at liberty to allege that an incriminating substance had been secreted into a white Cartier box on a table in the sitting room by Constable, who then enquired *sotto voce* how much it was worth to Jagger if the charge was dropped, naming a figure and adding didactically that a drugs conviction made things difficult if the miscreant wanted to work abroad.

Mick chose arrest. The consequent media coverage confirmed his and Marianne's status as a Scandalous Couple on a par with Serge Gainsbourg and – about to move from Cheyne Gardens to Cheyne Walk – Jane Birkin. These two were the makers of that summer's UK chart-topper, 'Je T'Aime...Moi Non Plus', on which an easy-listening arrangement seeped incongruously beneath grunts, moans and whispers as prospects of imminent sexual rapture increased towards the fade. Rising almost as high before the year was out, 'Melting Pot' – a plea for universal tolerance by the multi-racial Blue Mink – mentioned 'Mick and Lady Faithfull', its singer unaware of the disturbing erosion of the relationship.

Autumn leaves were falling too on Brian Jones's tenure with the Stones. Private anxieties and dark nights of the ego had long turned the easy affability of 1962 into vainglorious competitiveness with Keith and, especially, Mick. Worse than basking in a less dazzling spotlight was that Jagger, with Richards, had hogged a near-monopoly of songwriting within the unit structure. Brian's penetration of their caste-within-a-caste had been blocked further by the loss of the love of his life to it. After moaning ineffectually, he'd resigned himself to being treated as a tool for the masterworks of the fellows who'd once been his friends. Then, taking refuge in hard drugs, booze and other transient kicks, and reduced to just fretting guitar, Jones became not only expendable but a liability.

Jones and the group parted on 8 June 1969. A month later, he was face-down at the bottom of the swimming pool in the grounds of his retreat in the Sussex Weald, and the Stones' Hyde Park bash to mark the coming of Brian's replacement – Mick Taylor from

John Mayall's Blues Breakers – became 'tinged with black emotions, like everything else about the Stones', as Keith opined. 'You were constantly being drawn into the vortex of horrible events.'[10]

Following an oration by Mick for the drowned Brian, the five launched into two hours of hit-or-miss music. Among the hordes in the heat of the late afternoon in July, I couldn't recall much about individual numbers, only – and paradoxically – the claustrophobic midnight atmosphere that pervaded any given moment. The only remembered flash of levity was when somebody shouted, 'Oi, Mick! Do "Mona".' 'Yeah, we'll try and get to that,' replied Jagger, knowing that they never would. The buggers at the back couldn't see, but who cared about them? One determined soul clung to the top of a lamp-post for the duration.

During the 'Sympathy For The Devil' play-out and Jagger's departure by motorboat across the Serpentine, everybody near me was up, shoving and kicking, many of them trying to dance to the noise pouring from the PA. Limping to the Tube afterwards, I noticed two contradictory ideologies: a bootlegger checking his tape and some environmentalists clearing up litter, for which they were rewarded with virtue and a copy each of the Stones' new single.

Arch-feminist Germaine Greer could sneer that it was 'a kind of self-conscious slumming',[11] but 'Honky Tonk Women' was to be another Stones 'Best Single Of The Year' in 1969's *NME* poll. It was also at an opportune Number One in the US, and still in the Hot 100 when the Stones hit the road as a working band again for a major coast-to-coast assault on North America.

As well as alternating tracks from *Beggars Banquet* with a handful of golden oldies, the group premiered items from the album yet to come, *Let It Bleed* – 'out in about ten years' time', Mick had quipped at Hyde Park – notably 'Gimme Shelter'[12] and 'Midnight Rambler', the latter concerning a knife-wielding rapist.

Before they'd played so much as a quaver, blizzards of dollar bills had subsided into wads to pay for luxury suites, limousines, private jets and sufficient days off for Mick to gather the energy for what amounted to a nightly equivalent of the London marathon. 'I certainly don't want to go on stage and just stand there like Scott Walker and be ever so pretentious,' he laughed. 'I can hardly sing. I'm no Tom Jones, and I couldn't give a damn.'[13] Neither did the more personable groupies and other fabulous nobodies – aspiring to an orgasm at his thrust – whom he instructed members of the road crew to bring to his room, some to be gratified further by liaisons more enduring than a one-night stand.

Two could play at that game, however, and it reached Jagger's ears that Marianne – spending more time at her mother's in Aldworth these days than at Cheyne Walk – had embarked on more than a mere fling with Anita Pallenberg's old boyfriend, Mario Schifano. Yet Mick had clung on to the belief that she was worth keeping, even after a cry-for-help suicide attempt had prompted *Ned Kelly*'s insurers to insist on another as Jagger's leading lady in a production blighted further by objections about this *pommy poofdah* passing himself off as an Irish-Australian folk hero.

Other of the highly strung Faithfull's antics – her frank and public advocacy of free love, and her general involvement with the Stones and drugs – had already tarnished indelibly memories of the eternal sixth-former of 'As Tears Go By'. With Mick and Keith, she had also had a hand in composing 'Sister Morphine' – freighted with nightmare reflections and smelling pungently of hospitals – as the hastily withdrawn B-side of 'Something Better', her final 45 of the 1960s. 'Sister Morphine', she'd tell you, was not a veiled and morbid articulation of her own state – although she'd already had her first shot of the heroin that would ruin her looks and thus widen the abyss between her and Mick.

How much of a mockery, therefore, were their more recent shows of togetherness? At Marlborough Street Magistrates' Court, they'd held hands as she was acquitted and Jagger fined for possessing Detective Sergeant Constable's drugs, not quite a fortnight after the Stones had fled from the USA, emotionally exhausted through being out of their depth at Altamont, an outdoor bash intended to be a reconjuring in a different hemisphere of that sunny day in Hyde Park.

In a country where the black singer Nat 'King' Cole had been beaten up by racists midway through his act before an unsegregated Deep South audience, the collision of anti-heroes – the Stones and the Hell's Angels, the States' resident bad boys, employed as security – had turned the so-called 'West Coast Woodstock' into 'a horrible experience', as the entertainer at the centre of it all glared. 'Not so much for me as for the people that suffered.'[8] Chief amongst these was the fan with multiple knife wounds and profound bruising who died in the ambulance provided originally to whisk the Stones away after the concert.[14]

Occurring as it did in the final month of the Swinging '60s, indolent historians viewed it from a distance of decades as the end of an era, a final nail in the coffin of hippydom. 'It's all so wonderfully convenient,' scoffed a living relic of the age, who was also to help soundtrack the 1970s. 'Things aren't quite as simple as that.'[8]

10 Take Out Some Insurance

'I don't believe that each era is its own. I never imagined myself as part of Woodstock or anything like it. Nothing's over. Music is not over, nor any particular kind of it – nor its heyday.'

– *Mick Jagger*[1]

Among the immediate outcomes of Altamont was daily newspapers and the British music press making much of the symmetry of four deaths mitigated by four births during what was, on balance, a triumph for the main attraction. Even the *NME* was so ignorant of what actually occurred that it mixed up the 'long-haired blond youth' who'd thrown a punch at Jagger during the Stone's on-site walkabout the previous night with the murder victim, a Meredith Hunter, just some bloke fleetingly conspicuous when 'Mick came in for a spot of bother…but the ever-present Hell's Angels were on hand to deal with the intruder.'[2]

That was presumed to be that. Then the leaden skies over *Rolling Stone*'s block in San Francisco broke into a storm with the January edition's more subjective truth that Hunter had been slaughtered before the eyes of a frontman and his accompanists overwhelmed by the situation, the speed of events and their own 'diabolic egoism'.[3] Overall, Altamont had been no fun at all, and the Stones ought to, but didn't seem to, accept their major part of the responsibility – especially Jagger, who, raged Bill Graham, one of the tour's organisers, 'couldn't tell me you didn't know the way it would come off. I ask you what right you had, Mr Jagger, in going ahead with this free festival? What right do you have to leave the way you did, thanking everyone for a wonderful time and the Angels for helping out?'[3]

The experience was fading already for Mick, who – in public, at least – didn't seem particularly downcast by this bitter *adieu* to the decade that had defined him. In any case, a surge of personal anxieties had flooded the weeks surrounding *Rolling Stone*'s report. Marianne and Nicholas had met him at Heathrow when he arrived back from North America, via business meetings in Geneva. At Cheyne Walk, the old routine appeared to have been re-established as though Marsha Hunt, Mario Schifano *et al* had never happened, pardoned on both sides as passing fancies. Yet memories of the sufferance of life a couple of months before this emotional watershed remained fresh and couldn't be eradicated by hand-squeezing fondnesses. Into the bargain, John Dunbar had finally instigated divorce proceedings, in which Jagger was about to be named as third party.

When the *decree nisi* was granted to Dunbar, Jagger was ordered to pay costs. Motivated perhaps by worry about the case, an exuberance less unbottled than usual – as well as a general eschatological mood – was reflected in the reaction of a first-house audience 'totally lacking in energy'[4] when the Stones performed at London's Saville Theatre five days earlier. So Mick gloomed backstage in a troposphere of perspiration and tinted smoke while a member of one of the other outfits on the bill threw up into a washbasin.

The support acts exemplified vaguely both the passing of rock's old order and the advent of a new regime – or perhaps not so new. Mighty Baby had risen from the ashes of The Action, a mid-1960s outfit whose standing in Mod circles had been such that they'd be met on the outskirts of Brighton by a flanking cavalcade of Parka-clad scooter-riders to escort them to the venue. Deemed (possibly erroneously) a 'nice little band' of 'progressive' persuasion – and now as casually attired as the post-hippy onlookers – Mighty Baby were appreciated for their lengthy solos and clever ensemble playing – but not enough for the public to buy their two albums in sufficient quantities to prevent their disbandment within a year.

Entertaining a truer underground, up-and-coming provincial combo Shakin' Stevens And The Sunsets were a throwback to the Teddy Boys in both onstage garb and repertoire. Just as the widest river can be traced to many converging trickles, so a source of the impending return to the flashy glamour and cheap thrills of classic rock lies in precedents created by the likes of Stevens, Crazy Cavan And His Rhythm Rockers, US specialists Flash Cadillac And The Continental Kids and like outfits, who traded in premeditated reconstructions of times past.

That the Stevens combo gave a good account of themselves at the Saville belied a patronising *Melody Maker* critique, and was interrelated with a yet-unspoken weariness with certain subdivisions of pop that had emerged while the Swinging '60s petered out. Nevertheless, university undergraduates continued to squander their grants on gruff heavy metal, pretentious pomp-rock – and jazz-rock, of which Britain's leading executants were Colosseum, featuring Chris Farlowe, who invested the band's recitals with a much-needed element of humour. However, as with Mighty Baby, rather than separate pieces, it was almost the sound at any given moment that counted, for while there was no denying Colosseum's musicianship, it was more potent than much of the actual music.

However, the most anodyne of pop subdivisions was epitomised by the mannered, low-dynamic warblings of Crosby, Stills And Nash, America and similarly introspective individuals like James Taylor and his soon-to-be first wife, Carly Simon, and lesser acts that employed trudging 'laid-back' tempos and lyrics that made you embarrassed to be alive plus the apparently obligatory swirls of steel guitar that plagued every other album heard in blue-stocking hostel rooms.

When I was at college in the musically patchy early 1970s, I was gratified to discover that a few girls there preferred Shakin' Stevens And The Sunsets to Crosby, Stills And Nash. They hadn't so much as glanced at *The Once And Future King*. Tolkien left them stone cold. They'd never drawn flowers in felt-tip on scuffed white plimsolls, either. The Top 30 looked more hopeful, too, and would soon embrace supreme moments for also-ran veterans of the beat boom such as Marc Bolan, Alice Cooper, Slade, Gary Glitter, The Sweet and – most significantly – Bryan Ferry of Roxy Music and David Bowie. While the latter's first attempts at songwriting had aroused little enthusiasm, he was to become in middle age one of Britain's richest pop stars with a portfolio of compositions comparable in size and profitability to those of the Stones and The Beatles.

With Bowie in the producer's chair, Lou Reed – sounding tired rather than aberrantly 'laid back' – would enjoy chart success with singles on both sides of the Atlantic for the first time, although, however successful his solo output, it would always be measured against his music as leader of The Velvet Underground, who foundered without him and sundered in 1972.

Though able to carry on longer in a recognisable form, Canned Heat proved as incapable of major commercial or artistic recovery after Al Wilson's fatal drug overdose the previous year and a consequent flux of transient personnel.

White blues was arguably more alive and well in Britain. From High Wycombe, Brewer's Droop were perhaps the most alarming revivalists, specialising in an Anglicised form of Cajun with more than a dash of the hilarious filth that got them banned from many venues. With his foam-rubber phallus, vocalist Ron Watts was their Jagger – if a whiskered one with a wobbling beer gut – but Birmingham's Big Bear Records still saw much star potential in the Droop's ale-sodden outrage. The aptly titled *Opening Time* debut LP was a diverting encapsulation of their bawdy jocularity and musical predilections, but it struck the populous with 'the impact of a feather hitting concrete', shrugged Ron. The moment for a UK 'answer' to Canned Heat had passed, partly because the genuine article was now so *passé*.

Bob Dylan's time looked as if it was up, too. Following a lengthy withdrawal from pop in the late 1960s, it seemed that his 'comeback' had been a false dawn, on the evidence of 1970's mistitled *Self-Portrait*, heaving with playful non-originals; lacklustre *New Morning*; and a spot as a 1970s equivalent of 'featured popular vocalist' in George Harrison's star-studded Concerts for Bangla Desh at Madison Square Garden on an August Sunday in 1971. The coup of the decade for George would have been the reformation of The Beatles, but two – him and Ringo – out of four wasn't bad, together with Dylan, Eric Clapton and smaller big names doing their bit for the East Bengalis prostrated by both a cyclone and a reign of terror by a Moslem army mighty enough to eradicate the Hindu majority.

Newly domiciled in the south of France just days before the start of the financial year in April, a willing Mick Jagger was prevented from taking part in the spectacular because his visa couldn't be cleared in time. His reason for relocating to the Côte D'Azur wasn't the sunshine but because, despite the huge takings for the 1969 North American expedition, the Stones' revenue for the fiscal year had been overestimated. Expenditure exceeded income at a rate that couldn't cover a tax bill amassed over eight years of wrong assumption that such debts had been settled by their so-called advisors.

Suspecting that such an axe was about to fall, one of the purposes of Jagger's visit to Switzerland *en route* from Altamont to London had been to look into offshore banking deposits, investment funds and tax havens. His mind might have remained socialist, and his heart liberal, but, after supertax, his purse might not have been.

One possibility was the Channel Islands, traditionally a comfortable refuge for both financial institutions and individual fugitives from the incursions of the Inland Revenue and a Labour government fighting a formidable balance-of-payments deficit (inherited from the Tories) by credit-squeezing the rich. Moreover, as Crown dependencies, the archipelago offered an essentially English lifestyle in terms of language, currency and culture.

Eventually, the Stones acquired an office address on Sark, but the Mediterranean coast was attractive for being absent of cardiganed dotards tending roses, the meteorological whims of British summers and the empty hours between boarding-house teatimes and the pub. It was also more convenient as a base for touring and recording. The only fly in the milk-jug was the higher cost of living that had been the price of President de Gaulle appeasing France's seething workforce in summer 1968 with massive pay rises. As a result, a large white loaf that cost 1s 7d in the UK was six shillings in France, cooking apples were nearly twice as expensive as in Britain, and potatoes four times more. Lettuce, however, was cheaper, but man cannot live on lettuce alone.

Nevertheless, the Stones decided to go through with it, and commenced a 'farewell tour' of Britain. On the road, Mick read himself being put down as one more bourgeois liberal with inert conservative tendencies, while one twisted critic – damn his impudence – imagined he saw 'Jagger's tubby frame'[5] when the Stones materialised at the Marquee for the first time since 1963. In unconscious riposte, a sweeping exit from the land that bore him was crowned with the subject's teasing comment 'I can't see myself doing all this when I'm 30. I'll draw the line then.'[6]

After a sojourn in a Parisian hotel, Mick rented a well-appointed château, once owned by Pablo Picasso, in subtropical San Tropez, where whirring Nikons chronicled his comings and goings in the psychedelic-patterned trousers that seemed to clothe his legs in nearly every photograph from that period. Yet, while he conducted himself as if he'd been a *boulevardier* all his life, he missed the green fields and the cricket. Nevertheless, there was nothing else for it but to apply himself to getting a clearer picture from the confusion of an uprooting that would last at least a year.

At the heart of it was looking for a new record company. This was as chancy as looking for a new girlfriend, and now that the legal profession had insinuated its complex mumbo-jumbo into pop, deals couldn't be mapped out on a paper serviette over lunch any more (as, for example, Brian Epstein's had been with Billy J Kramer in 1963).

The expiry date of the Stones' Decca contract had been and gone the previous July; the only barrier to the Stones' complete freedom from the label being the delivery of one more single. This was relinquished via a burst of obscene nonsense entitled 'Cocksucker Blues', featuring just Mick and acoustic guitar at Stargroves on the Mobile,[7] the Stones' own portable recording studio. Then unreleasable, the master tape was not destroyed but locked in a safe, where it would lie as unforgotten as Serge Gainsbourg and Brigitte Bardot's cancelled 'Je T'Aime...Moi Non Plus' – the one that served as a useful demo for Jane Birkin – and *The Troggs Tape*, an illicit recording of a cross-purposes studio discussion riddled with swearing.[8]

Decca, nonetheless, clung to the hope that the Stones would re-sign, even in the teeth of washroom whisperings that Mick – the group's chief wheeler-dealer – had been noticed sharing a table with Atlantic's Ahmet and Nesuhi Ertegun in a London club. As the face of the hottest property in the industry now, Jagger was in a position to call shots about marketing procedure, which included the creation of the Stones' eponymous subsidiary label, bearing a logo that caricatured his own lips and tongue. 'We want to control prices to stop the price of records going up,' he demanded. 'I'd like to find new ways of distribution.'[9] If there was the slightest deviation from the ascribed riders and fringe benefits, wild horses wouldn't drag him out to utter one solitary syllable or sing a single note on a given album's behalf.

It was a tall order, but Atlantic was the label most prepared to obey, and there was also the enticement of its stable of black R&B artists, from The Coasters and The Drifters back in the 1950s to a bevy of chart-busting soul singers, among them Wilson Pickett and Don Covay. 'I think Mick would have liked to have been on

Excello,' confessed a half-serious Ahmet Ertegun. 'We were the closest he could get to Excello and still get $5 million.'[10]

While the Stones had reached an agreeable compromise between monetary gain and an affiliation to music that had captured a Dartford teenager's imagination, Atlantic recognised a sound investment as an autumn tour of Europe abounded with rushed stages, tear gas, injuries, arrests and a massive police security check at Hamburg's Ernst Merke Halle for 1,000 forged tickets. Moreover, as the trek reached its halfway point, Jagger punched an Italian journalist for 'asking stupid questions'.[9]

All this was grist to the publicity mill as the maiden 45 for Atlantic's Rolling Stones Records was in the shops a fortnight into the group's Gallic exile. A nascent version of horn-laden 'Brown Sugar' had been penned by Mick during the filming of *Ned Kelly*. Its verses effused images of slave ships bound from West Africa to US clearing houses, where cotton planters bought and branded the manacled cargo. Both below decks and in the stockades, the females were coaxed with whips into manifold lewd activities with their white captors. Black US politician Reverend Jesse Jackson urged the instant removal of 'Brown Sugar' from radio playlists as it sliced like a wire through cheese to a *Billboard* Number One.

An in-person slot on *Top Of The Pops* oiled the wheels of a comparable domestic climb. On the same show, the Stones also plugged its B-side, 'Bitch', and a ballad, 'Wild Horses', from the forthcoming *Sticky Fingers*, an album that absorbed just enough of prevailing fads not to turn off older fans. More than a touch of Santana – a Latin-America take on jazz-rock – prevailed in 'Can't You Hear Me Knocking', while 'Dead Flowers' sounded as if Jagger had inhaled the air around Nashville, the Hollywood of country music. A fashionable string arranger, Paul Buckmaster of The Third Ear Band – who'd opened the Hyde Park show – was summoned for 'Moonlight Mile' and perceived references to trendy stimulants that had caught on within the Stones' inner circle, and surfaced in the lyrics as regularly as rocks in a stream.

While 'You Gotta Move' was a roots-affirming rural blues from 'Mississippi' Fred McDowell, of greatest antiquity from the group's own portfolio was 'Sister Morphine', considered sufficiently venal for the substitution of another number on the album's Spanish pressing. There was also concern about the packaging in a sleeve designed by Andy Warhol. Like the protruding square of plastic on the cover of *Satanic Majesties*, a real zip on the fly of the denim-clad (and very obviously male) loins that graced the front of the album obstructed its snug insertion into a wire record rack.

Decca wouldn't have worn it, although after the loss of the Stones, the label realigned its scruples about the rejected cover submitted originally for *Beggars Banquet* – depicting a toilet wall festooned by Jagger and Richards in felt-tipped graffiti – by using it for *Stone Age*, one of many haphazardly programmed compilations of those Stones tracks they were entitled to release. This change of direction was exemplified too by August 1971's *Gimme Shelter* album, which almost resembled a mispressing with its cover shot from the recent Marquee bash[11] and its mingling of a handful of late-1960s items with excerpts from an Albert Hall recital in 1966.

Despite the Stones' sour-faced endeavours at damage limitation – which extended to posting music-journal adverts expressing their displeasure at these ragbags – both *Stone Age* and *Gimme Shelter* proved worthy marketing exercises. So was Mick's 'Memo From Turner' from the *Performance* soundtrack, teetering on the edge of the UK Top 30 after being issued as a Decca single in November 1970, six months after the US premiere of what *New Yorker* magazine – concurring with *Time* – denigrated as 'a humourless, messy mixture of crime and decadence and drug-induced hallucination'.[12] A testament to Rudyard Kipling's 'what should they know of England who only England know?', it faded from circulation to receive occasional showings in film clubs and art centres. Actually, it didn't last long at home, either, following a West End unveiling in January 1971 as a benefit for Release.

Seemingly, Jagger himself had lost interest too; photographers waiting to catch his red-carpeted entrance to both the cinema and the party at Tramps afterwards were disappointed by a non-appearance that also caused the more starstruck attendees to ask for their money back.

He was, so they gathered, fogbound in Paris with his latest flame, someone called Bianca.

11 Honest I Do

'I don't envisage a time when I shall ever get married and settle down. I might have kids and I might get married, but I'll never settle down. I'm not the type.'

– *Mick Jagger*[1]

One day at Cheyne Walk, an apparition had blown in from Berkshire. Swaying as if mildly intoxicated, it struggled to insert a key into the front-door lock. In the hallway mirror, it wasn't exactly fat, but it was overweight for its height. Its skin was pasty, its eyebrows were shaved and its hair cut close to its head. Female, it wore clothes that appeared to have been selected from those stored in its mother's attic in readiness for a jumble sale.

Letting herself go was all quite deliberate. It wasn't some kind of test to see if Jagger still loved her thus disfigured but a successful attempt by Marianne – whom Mick hadn't seen for weeks – to 'show I wasn't in the market any more'.[2]

Other changes weren't so calculated. Those closest to her noticed Faithfull half-closing her eyes as if in pain, fingers pressed against her temples, or lost in melancholy thought. Seeming to snap out of it, she would insist that nothing much was the matter, though nausea, dizzy spells, insomnia and bouts of depression were plaguing her persistently. She couldn't say specifically where it hurt most, only that it wasn't localised but seemed to hover all over. Marianne's wretched heroin odyssey had found its sea-legs, and junk mattered more to her now than growing old with Mick as two old friends who used to be lovers, relaxed about each other's amatory peccadillos while stepping ever closer to that bourne from which no traveller returns.

A free agent again, Mick no longer had to make even cursory attempts to hide his picking and choosing from the skirt that solicited him nightly, and his pursuit of suaver women. There'd be no one for the press to take seriously for several months – though the more trivial tabloids were itching to break the news about the paternity of Karis, a daughter born on 10 November 1970 to Marsha Hunt[3] on the National Health in St Mary's Hospital, Paddington. They were, however, more sure of themselves regarding Jagger's intimacies with Pamela Miller of Girls Together Outrageously – an outfit formed from Frank Zappa's domestic staff – and US actress Patti D'Arbanville, subject of a 1970 hit by Cat Stevens. There was also a romance with Carly Simon, immortalised, reputedly, in her 1972 million-selling single 'You're So Vain', with Jagger's voice obligingly to the fore during the choruses. There exists too an unreleased Simon version of 'Under My Thumb'.

To the dismay of those treasuring hopes of filling the void left by Marianne in Mick's life – and to the delight of the *paparazzi* – a tiny black cloud on the horizon darkened to a heaven-darkening tempest of certainty that he'd been struck by a metaphorical thunderbolt, just like that which hit the exiled Michael Corleone in the newly published novel, *The Godfather*. As it had been when the latter first clapped eyes on lovely Apollonia, Jagger wanted to possess Bianca Perez-Mora Macias from the moment they were introduced at a party on the executive floor of Paris's Hotel George V a few weeks before the coming of Karis.

Unquestionably, 21-year-old Bianca was a stunner in a slim-hipped, angular sort of way. Elegantly severe with little in the way of distracting jewellery, a flawless complexion was emphasised by the floridness of a full, almost fleshy mouth, not unlike that of Mick, who – in his favour – spoke fluent French. 'My big beauty secret is that I love and need lipstick,' she was to reveal. 'It makes me feel feminine even in dangerous circumstances, even in the middle of a war.'[4]

Though convent-educated and from a well-to-do Nicaraguan family, Bianca and her siblings' childhoods had been blighted by her parents' messy divorce and a homeland that had been under the thumb of three successive generations of the same autocratic First Family since 1936. Despots of a similar stamp to Hitler, the Somozas had secured the loyalty of hand-picked lackeys and funded the republic's army via money procured by extortion, gambling, prostitution and the plunder of the republic's treasury. Currying favour with the United States, the dictators were able to crush political opposition, high and low, without mercy. 'As a teenager, I felt powerless when I watched student massacres by Somoza's National Guard,' Bianca glowered. 'I also saw my mother being discriminated against as a divorced and working woman. From an early age, I learnt the meaning of discrimination, and aspired to make a difference, to become an instrument of change – but first I had to complete my education, so I applied for a scholarship to study political science in Paris.'[5]

Settling into campus life, she never lacked male attention, and was to cut a familiar and beautiful figure during a round of *soirées*, first nights and similar galas laced with the essence of fine tobacco and pricey perfume, functions where you'd pass up to a dozen cultural lions and showbiz personalities along a single staircase. Soon, she became scornful of the visible desperation inherent in the hysterical chatter, rehearsed patter and networking that accompanied such occasions. Nevertheless, it was through such ordeals of conviviality that Bianca acquired high-profile boyfriends, notably Michael Caine and, many years her senior, Eddie Barclay, chairman of an eponymous French-language record label with lucrative signings that included Charles Aznavour, Brigitte Bardot and Jacques Brel.

Barclay was still in the picture when Bianca came into the life of Mick Jagger. While she detected in him a strength of character lacking in other pop stars who'd hovered around her, he recognised a maturity beyond her years and a refusal to yield anything of her dignity and self-respect. Put crudely, Bianca was no 'hole in one'.

A fortnight's holiday together in Nassau, however, indicated that they were an 'item' by late autumn. Next came the expensive diamond bracelet he bought her and false denials by both – and their friends – that marriage was on the cards. 'He can't afford it,' chuckled John Lennon. 'The Stones would be all over.'[6]

12 May 1971 was the day named, at the shortest notice, for around 80 invitees – mainly relations and a who's who of pop illuminati – to be flown from London to St Tropez for ceremonies *en français* in both the council offices and a local Roman Catholic church. Divining what was going on, the world's media converged on the buildings, too, and the nuptials were almost postponed, so intrusive was the crush, inside and out.

How could anyone begrudge Mick and Bianca their joy at this Wedding of the Year? Annihilating completely any illusions he'd had about the Stones as agit-prop minstrels, Richard Neville dismissed such conformity not as maybe some sort of Dadaist concept but as 'the end of any further pretence of Mick Jagger as a figurehead of radical lifestyle'.[7]

Fuelling such condemnation, the no-expense-spared reception in a nearby theatre was marked by a procession of arriving Mercedes, Bentleys, Porsches and Rolls-Royces, and speculation about who could not be observed even opaquely behind their smoked windows. In the queue for the buffet, Ringo Starr nattered awkwardly with Paul McCartney, whom he hadn't seen since a blistering row the previous year. A former Walker Brother passed a plate of sandwiches to a member of Santana. Lord Lichfield shared the proverbial joke with Marshall Chess. Don't look now, but there goes Bardot! That chap I can't quite place – isn't he some French film director?

On the stage stood amplifiers and instruments in case any of those present felt an urge to entertain – as the groom did when the revels slipped into the graveyard hours. At around dawn, there was some tomfoolery by a swimming pool, some of the merry-makers being swung fully clothed into the chlorinated water.

As Charles Kingsley reminds us, 'Love can make us fiends as well as angels,' yet *Top Of The Pops* presenter Jimmy Savile's comments would be among those quoted on the flight back to England. 'After trying out the drug and permissive scene,' he ruminated, 'there's a lot to be said for the nice normal life after all.'[8]

It was very early days, but there wasn't any indication as yet that Mick intended to be routinely unfaithful to his bride, as he'd been to Chrissie and Marianne. Indeed, three was a crowd when their canoodling went beyond the bounds of acceptable ickiness on the honeymoon when, on evading a nosy world, they stayed at Venice's Hotel Gritti – 'the best hotel in Europe', according to fellow lodger Kit Lambert, then on a lonely holiday there. In Runyonese present tense, he added, 'The staff show Mick and Bianca into a room like a matchbox. It looks out onto a brick wall three feet away on the other side of the canal full of turds and cabbage stalks, so I intervene and say to them, "Look, if you don't mind sharing a drawing room, I have a spare double room, and you can have that." There they are, billing and cooing, and having shrieked at the sight of their matchbox, they gratefully accept when they see my four-poster and a balcony. I never see them, as they lock themselves in their room most of the time, but soon we get into the habit of having dinner together.

'When I leave, I nip down the night before and say, "I'll pay their bill." The next morning, I wake up and think I'm in Paradise – or at least in another room. It's got flowered wallpaper now – but when I'm fully awake, I realise that I'm surrounded by 24 dozen roses, red. They are arranged around the room and must have been put there while I was asleep in an hour or so. That takes some doing. Mick must have exhausted the entire contents of half a dozen flower shops in Venice.'[9]

The happy pair's first child, Jade, entered the world in a Parisian nursing home on 21 October 1971 – yes, I can count too – and among the fond smiles and baby talk an enraptured Mick commented jokily, 'When she grows up, I'll warn her to watch out for blokes like me.'[10]

As half of a celebrity couple, Jagger's name was cropping up more often in high-society gossip columns than *Melody Maker* these days. Famous for being famous, he and Bianca – both apart and, preferably, together – were desired guests at every glittering shindig, club opening, award ceremony, after-dinner laudation *et al* on the calendar. A poll of 2,000 international fashion editors placed them amongst the best-dressed men and women of 1972. There were overtures for both to star in movies, and Mick considered and then rejected a role in *Ishtar*, Donald Cammell's attempt at an update of a Bing Crosby, Bob Hope and Dorothy Lamour-type *Road* flick. Similarly, Bianca's more untried thespian abilities remained so when films by David Puttnam and, later, Andy Warhol didn't get far beyond discussion. The latter project drew from Mick a catty 'When girls get together, there's always talk, but they never get anything done.'[1]

Nonetheless, both the Jaggers consented readily to be photographed for the *Sunday Times* by Leni Riefenstahl, who shot the 1934 Nuremberg Rally (as *Triumph Of The Will*) and the Berlin Olympics two years after that. Her work for the Third Reich had been the making and then the ruin of her, and she had spent the decades since justifying it. Mick, however, found it 'amazing'[11] to be the cynosure of her lens. In turn, Riefenstahl was charmed to be pictured with Jagger, arms entwined.[12]

Everywhere he went, he was the focal point of eyes grateful to him for merely existing. If vibrantly gregarious with Bianca at the inauguration of G&M Records at the Ritz in Piccadilly, all he had to do to upstage founders of any feast there – or at Stringfellow's, Tramps, the Hippodrome, Regent Street's Café Royal and wherever else proprietors turned a blind eye to the snorting-up of top-quality cocaine in the toilets – was simply to go to them. Then everyone would stop sipping their poised cocktails as a muted buzz reached a whispered peak. This wasn't television or a centre spread in *Fabulous*; Mick Jagger – that impossible yardstick of teenage escapism and aspiration – was actually within, asserting his old power in abundance while the younger icons and their acolytes droned around him like a halo of flies.

In the smartest Los Angeles restaurant, even the coolest heads turned when Mr Jagger was conducted to a table for lunch with Rudolf Nureyev. By the same token, 'Bianca' was no longer a name noticed only by bored choirboys as the forename of Bianca da Siena, author of the Whitsuntide hymn 'Come Down, O Love Divine'. Nowadays too, baby girls were being launched into life as 'Bianca', most famously a ficticious one, who was to emerge as an adolescent in the television soap-opera *EastEnders*.

Wasn't that Bianca Jagger at Liza Minnelli's midnight concert at the London Palladium? There she was again in the Blue Hawaii Room of New York's Roosevelt Hotel at the anniversary of The Mothers Of Invention's first ten years in showbusiness. Meanwhile, her husband was in the Big Apple, too, at the reopening of the Bottom Line club, in a cluster with Stevie Wonder, Carly Simon and, looking rather down-in-the-mouth, James Taylor.

Mick was also inhabiting a world more cultivated than that of a pop socialite, spending a few summer weeks at, say, Lord Gowrie's pile in County Kildare. During an 'at home' at Cheyne Walk for his own people, Mick displayed an area of expertise usually associated with those born into privilege. Showing off his wine cellar to Gary Glitter and Faces guitarist Ron Wood, he spoke with much authority about different vintages and regions.

These days, he was professing that he didn't listen to much rock 'n' roll any more, either, and certainly none of the records that had made his schooldays more bearable. More worryingly – and perhaps because he'd heard of Scott Walker's cynical debut in supper-club cabaret – he was still thinking aloud about washing his hands of pop altogether when he reached his 30s: 'There's a time when a man has to do something else. I don't want to be a rock star all my life. I couldn't bear to end up in Las Vegas with all those housewives and old ladies coming in with their handbags.'[1]

Yet he wasn't above putting his head around the door at recording dates for Dr John (composer of 'Walk On Gilded Splinters') and John Lennon, going as far as contributing vocals to the former's *The Sun, The Moon And The Herbs* album and taping a rendition of Willie Dixon's ribald 'Too Many Cooks' to the ex-Beatle's chord strumming.[13]

Mick also saw the funny side of Keith Moon, The Who's madcap drummer, winning a bet that he could break into the Jaggers' 11th-floor hotel room. Clambering up the wall Spider-Man-style, Moon burst through the open window to face the barrel of a revolver that Mick – heart pounding like a hunted beast – pulled from beneath a pillow. Though startled from slumber too, Bianca subjected her spouse to an amused scolding for so alarming the intruder, before dressing, applying make-up and going dancing with Moon while Mick remained huddled, bemused, under the bedclothes.

Nevertheless, his wife's zest for the social whirl, his newly discovered sensibilities about the shallow rituals of pop and the initial conjugal bliss was creating friction as the Stones buckled down to a new album – a double – *Exile On Main Street*. There was particular concern about Mick's increasingly compartmentalised life causing him to vanish from the sessions, often on the slightest excuse, to be with Bianca.

While others in the group's coterie said nothing about a woman they thought rather intimidating, Keith Richards could not contain his resentment. The subtext, of course, was that Bianca had disrupted the old friendship. When she wasn't around, Keith would ease up, happy to have Mick's undivided attention again.

Gradually, however, there came if not a reformed Richards then a new mood. While not precisely genial, his manner towards Bianca became grimly urbane – or, at least, he chose to hide any animosity. However, on a flight to the States with the Jaggers and Anita, he couldn't prevent himself from drawing contentedly on a cigarette at Bianca's discomposure as the air turned blue during Mick's altercation about seating with an air hostess. You can take a man from Edith Grove, but you can't take Edith Grove from the man.

All the same, Keith had to admit that, whether Mick had pulled his weight during the actual recording or had found more interesting things to do, he went beyond the call of duty when *Exile On Main Street* was on point of release by composing and singing verses[14] that, with piano accompaniment, linked excerpts from the album on a flexi-disc given away with the *New Musical Express* on 29 April 1972. This – and Mary Whitehouse's complaints to the BBC about the lyrics to certain tracks – helped to ease the package's swift journey to the top of charts across the globe.

There would also be much to praise about Jagger's singing. 'Let It Loose' – 'the single most soulful thing the Stones ever recorded'[15] – was to earn him a placing in *Mojo*'s *100 Great Voices And The Records That Prove It*,[15] albeit with the qualification that he 'was never a Van Morrison (or even a Stevie Winwood), but he could pull out the stops when the song warranted it…pushing himself beyond his usual posturings'.

Written long after the fact, however, this critique bequeathed unto *Exile On Main Street* a flashback grandeur that belied 1972's 'very indifferent reviews', groaned Jagger, while agreeing that '*Beggars Banquet* and *Let It Bleed* were better records. They're more compressed. When you put a double album out, there's always going to be something that could have been left off. The truth is that it wasn't a huge success at the time. I'm being supercritical, but the record lacks a little focus.'[16] These remarks were made during another period when it wasn't all smiles between Mick and Keith – and it's not difficult to imagine the latter's knuckles whitening as he read them.

12 Baby, What You Want Me To Do?

'I don't think Mick needs to be so conscious of what the rest of the rock hierarchy are doing. He shouldn't take any points from himself as to what Bowie's doing or Led Zeppelin.'

– Keith Richards[1]

Some of Mick's high-born friends delighted in appalling staider swells by letting slip during after-dinner conversations that they'd entertained Mick Jagger and his missus last weekend at the mansion. Nice people, the Jaggers. He's got a Bentley, you know.

Yet, no matter how far up the social ladder Mick had climbed – especially since contracting what Bianca was to call 'my well-known marriage'[2] – he remained a long-haired rock singer, wilder and fouler than most others, and his job was to perform. So, after scheduling six weeks of concerts across North America, he buried his misgivings about the fallout from Altamont to the extent of establishing a concordat with Bill Graham, who was still grousing about the Stones' previous tour with bitter intensity.

Three days after opening night in Vancouver, the group ventured into 'Injun territory' – ie San Francisco, where Graham had let commerce rule finer feelings by booking them for his Winterland auditorium. Along some backstage corridor there, Jagger strode up to Bill, flashing a wide, eye-crinkling smile.

Appeased, the tetchy old promoter couldn't help liking Mick and wished the Stones well for the many dates left on the itinerary. Predictably, these did not pass without incident, most notably at

Montreal's Forum, where French-Canadian separatists planted a bomb underneath an equipment truck. The explosion delayed proceedings by several hours while replacement amplifiers and instruments were procured. Like a trouper, Mick was placid and even-tempered in the wings, as if there was no bedlam and no beer-can whizzing past Stevie Wonder's drummer's ear. After the headliners were introduced, the audience noise was fantastic, but Jagger seemed as unbothered by this as he was by suffering more feedback bleeps than usual, one of the sound crew blundering on to replace a dead microphone, some front-row girl bouncing her tits at him or her friend weeping loudly throughout. Even a glancing blow from a flying bottle couldn't stop the show for Mick, as flickeringly and groinally daredevil as ever. Back at Madison Square Garden, Bette Midler – then injecting archly *kitsch* cabaret into pop – was beside herself with excitement: 'I got out of my seat and I stood in the aisle, and I just saw what Mick Jagger was doing. Oh, the nerve! I stood there and I shouted, "Please, oh please!" Oh, how I wanted him!'[3]

Further representatives from showbusiness – as well as the worlds of politics, literature and even royalty – were joining the common herd filing into this civic arena or that baseball colosseum, not to listen to the hits and a few tracks from *Exile On Main Street*, but to take part in an uproarious tribal gathering. If 50-year-old Truman Capote, commissioned to cover the tour for *Rolling Stone*, was lukewarm about Mick's cavortings,[4] a person answering the writer's description was observed jiving tipsily by himself in the wings during 'Midnight Rambler'. The presence of other VIPs such as T-Bone Walker, Orson Welles, Bob Dylan, Andy Warhol, Ike and Tina Turner, Britt Ekland and assorted Kennedys – including Princess Lee Radziwill, Jackie's sister – tipped the balance for corner-cutting journalists on the national dailies. 'They were famous: now they are a legend!' gushed the *Chicago Sun-Times*,[5] agreeing at last – in so many words – with Andrew Loog Oldham's ancient sleeve notes that The Rolling Stones were, indeed, 'more than just a group – they are a way of life'.[6]

However, the Stones weren't on so high a plateau that they could afford to stop fighting the same battle as other acts on the same circuit: the battle for chart placings, the battle for bums-on-seats, the battle for money. The main enemy in the early 1970s was Led Zeppelin, who, rising from the ashes of The Yardbirds, specialised in the sonic pictures of high-energy, blues-plagiarised, Genghis Khan-esque carnage that were ideal for US stadia designed originally for championship sport.[7]

The late Peter Grant, the band's fearsome manager, was urged to sign older Stones rivals, The Pretty Things, to Led Zeppelin's own new Swan Song label. Hardship and disappointment had induced the Things to take a brief sabbatical (and compelled Dick Taylor not to re-enlist), but 1972's *Freeway Madness*, with its domination of riffs over melody, allowed them to remove themselves to the States, where – as Led Zeppelin had already realised – collegiate youth seemed fair game to buy anything British that was labelled 'heavy'.

'It was the first time we got some attention,' grinned Phil May. 'Led Zeppelin would fly in under assumed names to wherever we were and sit in the front row.' Relentless touring paid off, with both Swan Song albums appearing in the lower reaches of *Billboard*'s lists, and the Things enjoying prestigious second-billings to such as Bad Company, The Kinks and, at the bitter end, Uriah Heep. Often the Surprise Hit at this or that back-of-beyond European festival, too, there was a sufficiently firm substratum beneath pop's capricious quicksand to make it worth carrying on.

Had they wished, The Pretty Things might have made headway in glam-rock Britain, where ex-*Ready Steady Go* floor manager Paul Gadd had washed up near the top of the charts in 1972 with 'Rock And Roll Part 2', a primitive call-and-response chant to a quasi-military beat. Its success had come as much through Gadd's adoption of his 'Gary Glitter' alias and trademark silvery stage costumes. With much the same football-terrace appeal, further massive sellers – including a hat-trick of Number Ones – established Paul/Gary as overlord of glam rock, albeit fighting a rearguard action against T Rex, The Sweet, Slade, Bryan Ferry's Roxy Music and David Bowie.

Wondering at Glitter as he had at The Troggs[8] for a natural regression, as well as his 'use of clichés',[9] Mick Jagger had watched Gary open a rock 'n' roll revival spectacular at Wembley Stadium on 5 August 1972. Giving the lie to his assertion that he had no time for classic rock any more, Mick was snapped in the artists' enclosure chatting with proud familiarity to Chuck Berry prior to paying respects to Little Richard, remarking that he preferred 'Lucille' to the latest by Slade, whose A-side output was to consist mostly of unremitting ravers.

As well as providing a principal catchphrase on *Beggars Banquet*, Richard's 1966 single, 'Get Down With It' (as 'Get Down And Get With It'), had been Slade's maiden Top 20 entry. Richard was also fresh from a cameo on Canned Heat's tribute 45 'Rocking With The King'. It seemed to make sense, therefore, for him to climb aboard the nostalgia bandwagon, though it started badly when Richard's hippy peace signs, an interminable 'When The Saints Go Marching In' and – especially – his overt self-love were booed at Wembley.

Little Richard was merely stressing the glam elements he'd had from the beginning – as were The Faces, Lou Reed (who pioneered black male lipstick), The Kinks – and kohl-eyed, mascara'd Mick Jagger, always a little bit *femme* anyway, in the studded jumpsuit with its girly sash that he'd worn on the boards in North America. For a Far Eastern expedition in 1973, he'd sport a tiara, possibly to distract attention from hair cut rashly short.

If not boarding the glam bandwagon by any means, Mick was an automatic contender with one of Marsha Hunt's old *beaux*, Marc Bolan, whose talkative conceit on attaining renown with T Rex infuriated contemporaries. When he implied in the press that the squealing 'T Rexstasy' that attended his concerts was one in the eye for the Stones, Jagger scoffed that he was 'not interested in going back to small English towns and turning on ten-year-olds'.[10]

He was much the opposite of derisive about David Bowie, whose outrageous alter-ego 'Ziggy Stardust' – as well as a *Melody Maker* interview in which he'd made out that he was bisexual – had been the making of him. A longer term prospect than Bolan and Glitter, Bowie abandoned glam symbolically by announcing his 'retirement' – actually, the death of Ziggy – at the Hammersmith Odeon on Tuesday 3 July 1973. Mourners came to take a last look at the corpse at a lavish do in the Café Royal, where David – triumphant and supreme – greeted Mick like an old comrade, saving a seat on his right hand at the head of the dinner table. On his left, Lou Reed was also amenable to being photographed in a group hug with the three stars kissing each other to the applause of Keith Moon, Cat Stevens, two ex-Beatles, Barbra Streisand and the rest of the crop harvested by Bowie's investors.

A continued amity had Jagger and Bowie – a Kentish Londoner, too – talking tirelessly on the telephone like teenagers, even though David and Angie, his wife, lived literally just around the corner from Cheyne Walk. The two men were sighted on companionable outings – with and without Bianca and Angie – to, say, catch Diana Ross at the Royal Albert Hall or, in April 1973, watch Muhammad Ali's defeat by Ken Norton in San Diego.

Christmas came, and David gave Mick one of the first privately purchased video cassette recorders in Britain, but received 'something like a tie'[11] in return. Overspending had never been Jagger's way. Even so, he was close enough to Bowie to seek guidance about the uncertain future of the Stones when, on inviting his pal to the Newcastle stop of a British tour the previous September, the group had lost the attention of a faction within the crowd who, spotting David's bottle-orange plumage, had gawped at him rather than the stage.

A mutual-admiration society, Jagger and Bowie praised each other in print, Mick considering David – unlike Gary Glitter – to be 'a very serious artist'.[12] On his first post-Ziggy album, *Aladdin Sane*, Bowie sang of 'Jagger's eyes' in 'Drive In Saturday' and rehashed the 1967 Stones A-side, 'Let's Spend The Night Together' on side two.

If deploring the general quality of Mick's lyrics, Bryan Ferry exhumed 'Sympathy For The Devil' in quasi-'Monster Mash' fashion on a 1973 solo LP. He was on a par with Bowie as a Jagger for the 1970s, via an image that was a collision between the acme of elegance as a singing pianist and a studied, if endearing, centre-stage gawkiness via the kind of gyrations that a managing director might try when dancing an embarrassed Twist with a voluptuous typist at the office party.

Roxy Music didn't make much headway in the States, and Bowie's first Top Ten entry was a long time coming, but the Stones were sure enough of their standing there to let 1973's *Goat's Head Soup* album fend for itself without any accompanying tour. The only appearance on that particular landmass that year had been January's hastily organised fundraiser at the Los Angeles Forum, held in support of the refugees of a Yuletide earthquake in Nicaragua's capital, Managua – where many of Bianca's relations still lived. Tremors could be felt all along the spine of Central America.

Gathering together a mere fraction of the medicines and further foreign aid needed to cope with the disaster, Bianca and her man's shocked inspection of the aftermath of homelessness and disease prompted the Stones to take a giant leap for Managua. Moreover, the Jaggers' personal resources poured forth more than the Forum show netted, which itself generated a greater amount than George Harrison's Concerts For Bangla Desh. The delivery of the cash, however, was hindered by turgid US bureaucracy as well as interference from the affected country's corrupt government.

While Bianca appealed directly to the US Senate, Mick arranged a charity auction of Stones memorabilia days before the group's trek around Australasia and the Far East, troubled by every fibre

If professing a dislike of physical exercise, Mick (back row, extreme right) was a luminary of Dartford Grammar's Basketball Society

Mick's bass-playing cousin, Rick Huxley (extreme left), as a member of The Dave Clark Five

Photograph courtesy of Rex Features

When still amenable to stage costumes, (left to right) Keith, Charlie, Brian, Mick and Bill endorse Vox amplifiers, July 1963

The hour and the man: Jagger at Wimbledon Palais, 1964

Photograph courtesy of Jacqueline Ryan

Photograph courtesy of Jacqueline Ryan

Keith Richards, 1964: 'Very much in his own world,' said Ronnie Spector

Mick and his first celebrity girlfriend, Chrissie Shrimpton, return to London after holidaying in Jamaica, December 1964

Chris Farlowe, Mick's chart-topping production client, on *Ready Steady Go*, 1966

Marianne Faithfull, Mick and (obscured in spectacles) Stones minder Tom Keylock outside Malborough Magistrates Court, 29 May 1969

Bryan Ferry claimed that his romance with Jerry Hall was over long
before she and Jagger became an 'item' in 1977

Mick (left) in 1980 with brother Chris and father Joe. Twenty years
later, the sons sang a spiritual at mother Eva's funeral

Jagger, father and son, at Buckingham Palace with Karis and her half-sister, Elizabeth (right) after Mick was knighted by the Prince of Wales on 12 December 2003

(Left to right) Dick Taylor – former Rolling Stone and present-day Pretty Thing – with the author and 'God of Hell fire', Arthur Brown, May 2004

With Jude Law at the New York premiere of *Alfie*, a remake of the Swinging Sixties sex-comedy. 'Old Habits Die Hard', the Jagger single from the soundtrack, was poised to enter autumn 2004's UK Top 40

of red tape that could be accumulated to prevent these decadent *ketos* from defiling Japan. When questioned then by a US rock scribe if the Stones ever used drugs, Jagger had replied, 'No, never,'[13] but since 1969 he'd resumed a habit – noted by one fellow traveller – of having a supply of cocaine to hand, although onstage perspiration no doubt diminished its effect. Even so, 'I never saw him doing heroin.'[14]

Such allegations, however unsubstantiated, were not conducive to an easeful passage around the globe. Neither was Jagger's proposal for their next single, a *Goat's Head Soup* ditty with a title derived from its charming hookline: 'Starfucker, starfucker, starfucker, starfucker, sta-ar!' The cut was vetoed by Atlantic, and Radio 1 presenter Anne Nightingale's producer was reprimanded when, renamed 'Star Star', it had been spun inadvertently the evening before the album's domestic release was heralded by a publicity garnering knees-up in the cafeteria of Blenheim Palace, with Mick and Bianca sweeping in to an orgiastic clicking of shutters.

The most baleful spectre at the feast was Marianne Faithfull, now in the legion of the London pavements' loneliest, most alienated people: mainlining heroin addicts and their pushers, meths drinkers, beggars and other down and outs, some boasting of influence over a public-toilet attendant as a *bon viveur* at the Ritz would over the head waiter.

It hadn't taken long for Marianne's glide on pop's strongest winds to seem like a previous existence. It was monstrous and – in the days of her lightweight 1960s hits – unthinkable, but her deterioration had driven her to a shameless day-by-day pitch on a low wall near the dazzle of Piccadilly, at the mercy of the seasons. Morning became evening as she sat in a languid daze induced by either the drug of diminishing returns or the fixity of waiting for a fix. Sometimes, in a strange if dull euphoria, there was a vague enchantment in imagining that her vigil would be endless. Later, she'd bury her face in wet hands to the faint sound of deep sobbing.

The final scene of a 15-act tragedy might have been her wretched demise while dwelling in cardboard-boxed squalor with the vagrants around Euston, Waterloo and the Elephant and Castle. After the bonfire shrinks to embers, the chill from the misty river penetrates her frayed and grubby clothes, the height of made-to-measure fashion when she was with Mick, but now crumpled further after another sleepless night.

Yet, however low Marianne sank during these wilderness years – or wilderness 18 months, to be precise – there was the safety net of going home to mother, once she'd calculated how long she could be away from the wall and heroin, as well as Good Samaritans like Brion Gysin, a painter connected to the Chelsea Set, 'one of the few who came to find me when I was living on the street'.[15]

This gloomiest chapter in Faithfull's career was nearing a hospitalised close when, in June 1973, another of Mick Jagger's former lovers applied for child support via a reluctant affiliation order. Privately, he had acknowledged paternity of Marsha Hunt's daughter, welcoming Karis and playing with her on the rolling lawns of his Côte D'Azur spread when Bianca was expecting Jade. However, when Marsha brought the girls' kinship to public light, it sparked his sardonic implication that it was a publicity stunt by one whose single 'The Beast Day' was about to harry the German Top 40.

You could understand his attitude towards Hunt, whose stage appearances – fronting a group drawn from the ranks of The Poets, one of Immediate's signings – was prefaced by a spin of a 1973 hit by The Temptations, 'Papa Was A Rolling Stone'. Nevertheless, Jagger knew and Marsha *knew* that he knew that legally ordained monthly maintenance payments were inevitable after he'd gone through the motions of a blood test.

At Marsha's flat in St John's Wood, Karis's second birthday party had been attended by Jade. Her ringlets contrasted with the host's waviness, but otherwise the two were as alike as half-sisters could be. Karis would also be able to reconjure childhood memories of Cheyne Walk and the discs that shook the stereo there. In 1973, a turntable fixture was reggae, both well known and obscure. To Gary Glitter, Jagger seemed as knowledgeable about this as he was about wine: 'Again, he was an expert, and started explaining what was going on inside the rhythms and commenting on little subtleties of the mix.'[16]

As Keith was, if anything, even more passionate about reggae than Mick, nothing would do but the Stones had had to repair to Kingston, Jamaica, to record *Goat's Head Soup*. Between hotel and studio, they may have gazed from car windows at the city's poorer quarters, with their dirt-poor shanties and reeking squatters' camps rife with sickness and swarming with under-nourished children descended from the black slaves at the lyrical core of 'Brown Sugar'. Mixing business with pleasure, the Stones may too have been shown a good time in local clubs. Even so, the stay in Kingston wouldn't leave a pronounced mark on *Goat's Head Soup*'s pot-pourri of old ideas.

'Dancing With Mr D',[17] for instance, was a sequel to 'Sympathy For The Devil', while 'Hide Your Love' – with Jagger singing to his own piano-pounding – wasn't unalike Boogie Bill Webb's 1952 country blues 'I Ain't For It' in both content and delivery. A time-honoured strategy of using a girl's forename as a title – as exemplified by 'Ramona', 'Charmaine', 'Peggy Sue', 'Claudette', 'Diane', 'Juliet', 'Michelle', 'Clair' and so on – was employed for 'Angie', the ballad that was the album's first single, and a US chart-topper to boot.

The release of 'Angie' also stirred up an immediate – and ill-founded[18] – rumour that it was a paean to Mrs Bowie. Was Jagger up to no good with her? She insisted that he wasn't, but recalled serving breakfast in bed to him and her David after the previous night's roisterings had rendered Mick unwilling to negotiate the few minutes' dawdle back to Cheyne Walk. There was conjecture about an affair, and David was to confess that he found Mick 'incredibly sexy and very virile'.[11] Had Jagger been persuaded to experiment for much the same reason as Serge Gainsbourg, who'd freely admitted that, yes, he'd once had a homosexual experience, 'so as not to remain ignorant'?[19]

More stomach-knotting perhaps for Bianca was her husband being talked of (and written about) with women, among them singer Dana Gillespie – one of David Bowie's former girlfriends – as the old antagonism between fidelity to one's mate and the allure of the forbidden eroded the marriage as certainly as it had every other love that he'd thought would last for ever.

13 Shame Shame Shame

'I got married for something to do. I've never been madly, deeply in love. I wouldn't know what it feels like. I'm not an emotional person.'

– Mick Jagger[1]

The Jaggers spent 1974's summer on Andy Warhol's Long Island estate, where the late pop artist screenprinted an image of Mick in the same recurring style as his more widely exhibited portraits of Elvis Presley, Jacqueline Kennedy, Marilyn Monroe and Elizabeth Taylor. Warhol and Jagger were to autograph 250 portfolios of ten each for sale. They weren't cheap – and neither was the rent on the house in the same vicinity, where Mick and Bianca dwelt, initially, from September to October.

As leaves turned brown, marital bonds continued to loosen, but the pair still tended to keep pace with each other's caprices, being photographed at the same premieres and covering the same exhibitions, although Bianca was becoming increasingly disdainful about what she regarded as the shallowness of his cultural tastes, provoking an indirect riposte in his composition of a song entitled 'It's Only Rock 'n' Roll (But I Like It)'.

Although Mick's extramarital antics were provoking more direct exchanges between them, Bianca was putting a brave face on stray gossip-column mutterings, seeming to accept that 'my husband sleeps with many women' – dropped airily into a *Sunday Express* interview[2] – explaining, as much to herself as anyone else, that such promiscuity had no effect on Mick's emotional allegiance to the mother of his second daughter. She wasn't so naive to presume that he hadn't succumbed to temptation by camp-following floozies while in other hemispheres.

In turn, Mick shrugged off her alleged accumulation of bills for costly objects she couldn't see without wanting to possess. Neither did he mind male companions – such as Austrian actor Helmut Berger; Jack, the right-on son of US President Ford; and the harmless Warhol – all accompanying Bianca, almost like 18th-century *cavalieres servantes*, to any social occasion that he was unable to attend. Some of them, however, tired of always meeting her in public.

However, the dilution of his marriage wasn't as pressing a matter as that of the Stones' business relationship with Allen Klein. Long gone were the days of any open-handed conviviality around his desk. 'Klein would probably sue if I told you my opinion of him,' snarled Jagger. 'He's a person to be avoided, as far as I'm concerned.'[3] Just as Mick had said he would, George Harrison was – to put it politely – also having doubts about the so-called 'Robin Hood of pop'. Klein had been increasingly less available since the Bangladesh shows, and headlines like *Rolling Stone*'s 'Did Allen Klein Take The Bangladesh Money?' were not reassuring.[4]

The stench of corruption – more pungent than usual – was so pervading the entire industry then that a US television news channel compiled a one-hour special, *The Trouble With Rock*, which placed dirty dealings in the music business on a par with the winkling out of guilty secrets that had led to President Nixon's resignation. Present as a talking head on the programme, a mediatory Mick was 'sure there's other industries in America that are far dirtier than the record industry',[5] but the accusations – however unfounded – about Klein and Bangladesh renewed the Stones' protracted determination to curtail the fellow's handling of their affairs, both during and after his official tenure as manager. For instance, he remained *de facto* controller of remaindered recordings from the dear, dead Swinging '60s, some of which had been prised from

Decca's vaults for issue in various formats since 1971, the most recent being a single of the 'Out Of Time' that combined Mick's vocal and Chris Farlowe's backing track.

By one of those odd coincidences that periodically impinge on pop, 'Out Of Time' fought two simultaneously released revivals (by Nazareth's Dan McCafferty and by Arthur Brown), as well as a re-promotion of Chris Farlowe's version, for the fleeting grip on the UK Top 50,[6] which nevertheless gave Farlowe's bank account a welcome shot in the arm. Since the sundering of Colosseum, all signposts pointed to the snowballing nostalgia circuit for Chris. As his distant friend Mick could have advised him, a mere Great Voice wasn't enough to sustain contemporary interest.

Since when has pop obeyed any law of natural justice? Not yet fallen from such grace were lesser vocalists like Joe Cocker, who, nonetheless, had finished below Mick Jagger in that year's World's Greatest Vocalist musicians' poll in the *NME*. Meanwhile, while Mick had failed to beat John Lennon, Paul Rodgers of Free and Bob Dylan, he had tied at fourth with Maggie Bell, a hard-faced Glaswegian contralto of gutbucket persuasion.

He could still take Top 30 strikes for granted, too, if not Number Ones. As a 1974 A-side, 'It's Only Rock 'n' Roll' hadn't sold millions, but had crept to Number 18 in the States and, in the wake of an orchestrated graffiti campaign across London, reached the Top Ten – just – at home, becoming briefly something of a national catchphrase. It also triggered an affectionate parody in 'It's Only Knock And Know-All' at the climax of *The Lamb Lies Down On Broadway*, a 1974 album by Genesis, whose chief showoff, Peter Gabriel, asked rhetorically, 'Is there a man alive who hasn't performed his Jaggerisms in front of the mirror? I know I have.'[7] More apparently, so had other vocalists high and low in the stadium-rock hierarchy, including Alice Cooper, Roger Daltrey, Ozzy Osbourne, Pete French of Cactus and Led Zeppelin's Robert Plant.

There had been no chances to witness an in-person masterclass for more than a year after the final date of 1973's European tour in October. The *It's Only Rock 'n' Roll* album wasn't taken on the road, and there was a distinct possibility that the follow-up – if it was ever completed – wouldn't be, either, owing to an unexpected vacancy. Out of the blue, Mick Taylor had written a formal letter of resignation, which was about his person when he, Jagger and The Faces' Ron Wood watched Eric Clapton play at the Hammersmith Odeon before drinks at Clapton's manager's home. Thus Taylor earned the distinction of being the second ex-member of the group with the same surname.

It would have been uncool to have shown any kind of consternation either at the *soirée* or when goaded about it by the media after the news broke. However, it was to be a long and sometimes mind-stultifying chore to prune down a formidable list of possible replacements. Although Alexis Korner was present at studio dates on the continent that served as auditions, among those under serious consideration were Robben Ford, whose squittering wah-wah had enlivened George Harrison's only solo tour; Leslie West, another rated American, on whose latest album, *The Great Fatsby*, Jagger had strummed rhythm guitar; Mick Ronson, David Bowie's Yorkshire-born guitarist; Dave Clempson, once mainstay of Colosseum; and a detectably balding Steve Marriott, esteemed by Keith Richards as a stronger singer than Jagger, who, insisted Steve, 'didn't want to play ball'.[8] While he added that he valued artistic freedom to superstardom anyway, Alexis's son Damian maintained that this assertion was contrary to Marriott's fervent desire to be a Stone.

For a while, Mick favoured former Yardbird Jeff Beck, who wasn't unwilling to give the Stones a try at a complex in Rotterdam early in 1975 – at least, until Beck 'couldn't handle it because my mind wasn't into that way of doing things. I was working a million miles an hour compared to the way they were.'[9] Now one of few rock guitarists capable of playing jazz-rock fusion convincingly, Jeff was impressed that the Stones had cajoled eminent hard-bop saxophonist Sonny Rollins to jam with them, but wasn't able to get used to two or even three of the principals being either very late or absent altogether from any given session.

Besides, when understanding more precisely what he'd be taking on, 'the sudden realisation that I might be a Rolling Stone frightened the hell out of me'.[9] Rather than informing them face to face, he pushed a note reading 'Sorry lads, I got to go home' under the door of Jagger's hotel room: 'I hated to do it because Mick's such a lovely guy.'[9]

The situation was resolved temporarily by borrowing Ron Wood from The Faces for the duration of a 1975 US tour that paralleled one by market competitors Led Zeppelin. North America was the only territory where either group could slip easily into a profit position far beyond the break-even point that was the norm in Europe. From the Times Square billboard to the chartered flights to the glossy full-colour programme to the wages of the lowliest equipment humper, the dollar outlay was in millions, but you also made millions.

However, contemplation of cost wasn't why Jagger's voice was spiced to agonised poignancy during the dress rehearsal on 21 May. Rather, it was the pain of a hand injury requiring 20 stitches, sustained three days earlier when the singer had been negotiating the circular glass door of a Long Island restaurant. Known to have performed with a streaming cold in the past, he insisted that the first show – at Louisiana State University a fortnight later – was not to be cancelled. Well, he didn't sing with his hand, did he?

A plaster cast hadn't been necessary, and a bandage wasn't visible from the mixing desk when, after a uniformed percussion ensemble ended a lengthy and enthusiastic tattoo, Mick trooped on with the others to a taped 'Fanfare For The Common Man' by Aaron Copland, as North American as Benjamin Britten was English. Jagger was also principal advocate of the 360-degree stage with 'no obstructive view. The people at the back can see. They get a fantastic view because the sound is all hung from above – and it sounds better too because it's directional sound.'[7]

Among less grandiloquent visual effects, the most memorable were the huge silk banners undulating in the air-conditioned breeze; a confetti-spitting serpent threading its way through the crowd; and the centre-stage inflation of a 20-foot long white penis. Wavering like a caber about to be tossed, this was a refinement (if that's the word) of Brewer's Droop's portable one. It didn't always achieve a full erection, owing to technical glitches, but this was laughed off by Mick – pretending to coax it from flaccidity – as an occupational hazard of 'mass funny entertainment. It's like an un-art event.'[7]

Reaching newspaper stands before the trek was a month old, the arch-conservative *National Star* wasn't remotely amused by Jagger and his prop, imploring, 'Where have we failed that this simple-faced disciple of dirt is a hero to our kids? We have this pale-faced foreigner getting ten dollars a seat from our kids to see him perform. And what do they see? They are blitzkrieged by a tightly packaged excess of four-letter words and tacky smut.'[10]

The journal took a similarly dim view of Jagger and Ron Wood 'doing this sort of David Bowie and Mick Ronson routine',[11] grinned the former, although Mick wasn't so crass as to copy his friend's simulated buttock-clutching fellatio on the guitarist's strings. However, his continuity embraced in-yer-face references to the sexual leanings of Billy Preston, a black Texan whose pedigree stretched back to stints as Little Richard's organist and in the *Shindig* house band; appreciation by other artists as a 'musician's musician'; a UK chart debut produced by George Harrison; and a continued solo career as a singer that had spawned two US Number Ones.

Prefaced by some scripted ad-libbing, Preston, as the troupe's musical director, was permitted to extricate himself from his bank of keyboards to give 'em a couple of numbers, replete with fancy footwork and soulman exhibitionism, while Mick took a breather. 'The audience needs a curve with a slight lull in the middle,' he elucidated. 'Otherwise they wouldn't have the energy for the end of the set.'[11] More of a lull than Billy was 'Little Red Rooster', heard last on the boards in 1965. Meanwhile, 'Get Off Of My Cloud', 'You Can't Always Get What You Want' and even an *a cappella* vignette of 'Lady Jane' were among further good old good ones.

His self-confidence boosted by the sleeve credit on *The Great Fatsby*, Mick also played guitar onstage for the first time, and was complimented on his chord-slashing by Jack Ford, who turned up at the Washington, DC, stop in the company of Andy Warhol and Bianca. Elsewhere, Raquel Welch, Charles Bronson, Olivia Newton-John, Diana Ross, Liza Minnelli and Ringo Starr received ovations as they were shepherded to their reserved seats.

The Stones' arrival in Los Angeles coincided with Starr's birthday celebrations. He was then resident in Santa Monica, separated from his wife and attempting to stay the phantoms of creeping middle age with hard drinking and waking in strange beds. A spent force artistically if not commercially, it was enough, he supposed, that he'd survived Beatlemania. One telephoned death threat had been taken so seriously, he said, that a detective had hunched beside the drum rostrum throughout a 1964 concert in Montreal, so he appreciated the worry of another still in the throes of perhaps the most unique human experience of the century.

Jagger's concerns were justified, recalling as he did the close shave that was Altamont and the backlash of opprobrium that crackled still. More recently, a 'fan', maddened by his girlfriend's more-than-passive interest in Frank Zappa, barged in front of the footlights at a London theatre to hurl the Mother Of Invention into the pit, confining him to a wheelchair for almost a year. On the near horizon was a certain David Littlejohn's authorship of a novel entitled *The Man Who Killed Mick Jagger?*

However, a vision of Mick sinking onto the floor with blood puddling from him, while ticket-holders who believed it was part of the act gave him an ovation, had been insufficient reason for the Stones' 1975 tour to be cancelled, any more than his gashed hand had been. Nevertheless, a firework that exploded one night as 'Sympathy For The Devil' cranked into gear, gave everyone a horrified start, but all's well that ends well, and beneath repeated announcements that 'The Rolling Stones have left the building' soft orchestral muzak oozed from the speakers while the customers streamed out onto the streets.

For those who hadn't taken *National Star*'s sermon to heart, the 'pale-faced foreigner' had been worth every cent. Yet the spectacle of his caperings with Keith and Ron bucking and lungeing about him couldn't mask mistakes and deficiencies preserved unforgivingly on bootlegs. He was still no Scott Walker, true enough, but who wanted Mick Jagger to be an amazing vocalist? 'The important thing about singing is to get the personality across,' he himself protested. 'Forget the notes.'[12] The veins in his forehead throbbed with effort, and lyrics and attendant moods were sold with questionable pitching to an involved audience in the midst of 'a noise we make, that's all. You could be kind and call it music.'[13]

By early autumn, when it was all over bar the shouting, the perpetrators looked at each other, shrugged their shoulders and banked the dollars netted. Apart from Ron Wood who within the week would embark on what turned out to be The Faces' last hurrah, thus freeing him to enlist as a full-time Stone, they took well-deserved holidays; Mick flying Bianca to Ireland to see if matters could be mended.

Whether in small paragraphs or half-page articles, the sunshine and showers of the marriage were being chronicled by the tabloids on an almost daily basis, with most tittle-tattlers alighting with nitpicking hope on the slightest indication of a drift into open estrangement.

14 Can't Stand To See You Go

'I'm not really working enough. It seems to come and go. Sometimes, you're working very hard. Then there are other times I just don't bother, and I get kind of impatient with myself.'

– *Mick Jagger*[1]

Dazzled by a paparazzo's flashbulb amid the mêlée of Mick's wedding, his mother had cried, 'I hope my other son doesn't become a superstar!'[1] Yet Chris Jagger had not retreated from public life since smelling the greasepaint in Israel. Milking his surname as much as his talent, G&M Records furnished his career as a solo artist with both the best and worst start in 1973 by issuing Chris's wryly titled *You Know The Name But Not The Face* album debut with a sleeve credit for brother Mick, prominent on the very opening track.

The Stones effused further from the speakers via the use of Ian Stewart and various of their auxiliaries, plus the Mobile. Finally, Chris could do nothing about his facial and vocal resemblance to Mick any more than Julian Lennon could about his to father John. A spin-off Chris Jagger 45 bit the dust, but G&M persisted with countrified *The Adventures Of Valentine Vox*, and Chris attempted a third LP with members of The Flying Burrito Brothers before returning to the theatre.

During this relatively slumberous period for the Stones, Chris's elder sibling was pondering once more whether memorising lines and putting up with the early starts involved in movie acting was worth the effort. Well, it had been a long time since *Ned Kelly*, even if Mick was in less of position to pick and choose – but it was the same for Elvis Presley, who was then supplicating Barbra Streisand for the opportunity to play opposite her in the romantic melodrama *A Star Is Born*. Apparently, Nicholas Roeg had considered Jagger for the titular space alien in *The Man Who Fell To Earth*, but 'he's too strong, too positive. I want somebody who looks as if he hasn't any bones in his body.'[2] The job went to the more feyly mysterious David Bowie, just as the one in *A Star Is Born* did to the more orthodox singer/songwriter Kris Kristofferson. Reputedly, Mick was actively chasing the role of 'Frank N Furter' in the film version of *The Rocky Horror Show* until it was given to Tim Curry. Hearsay implied too that Jagger was shortlisted to be Salieri, second lead in the Mozart bio-pic *Amadeus*.

Bianca's celluloid ventures were, if anything, fractionally more palpable. Riding roughshod over waspish press imputations such as 'If she weren't married to Mick Jagger, she'd be scrubbing kitchen floors',[3] she reached the showbusiness pages of some newspapers, pictured in a Parisian studio shoot for the subsequently abandoned *Flesh Coloured*.

Eventually, Bianca actually made it onto the silver screen in *The Cannonball Run*, a comedy hinged less on a plot than a series of themed sketches, whose lack of substance could not be disguised with a large budget and the employment of other famous names such as Roger Moore, Peter Fonda and Dean Martin. The same was true of 1978's *All You Need Is Cash*, a parody of The Beatles' fairy tale, in which Bianca – and her spouse – had cameos.

As neither Bianca nor Mick were the sort to wash dirty linen in public, nothing suggested that the couple's seemingly free-and-easy life together was anything less than tolerable. As late as November 1977, Bianca bid successfully at a pop-memorabilia auction at Sotheby's for a Cecil Beaton photograph of Mick, who in turn bought her a white horse and joined in the fun at her 33rd birthday celebration in Studio 54, where she made a grand entrance on the beast, led by a negro muscle-man naked but for glittery green woad and a fig leaf.

As for Mick's other women, it wasn't as if mistresses and one-night stands were uncommon, even in Britain, although it was a Gallic homily that ran, 'The chains of marriage are so heavy that it takes two to carry them, and often three.' Bianca wasn't averse to a little frivolity either, and there were plenty of good-looking and amusing men looking for a bit of frivolity, too.

Hunched over their typewriters, 'creative' journalists wondered whether to tease some column inches from Bianca pecking the cheek of Bob Marley – 'the Mick Jagger of reggae'[4] – during a post-concert carouse in Paris's Club Elysées Matignon, but chose instead to intimate that her flirtings with David Bowie, film actor Ryan O'Neal and tennis champion Bjorn Borg had taken serious turns. Bianca denied these liaisons just as Mick did with…oh, let's see: US celebrity photographer Annie Leibovitz, girlie-magazine pinup Bebe Buell and any number of pop and Hollywood starlets.

Evidence that he and Bianca were over was most tangible when they were sighted sitting at separate tables in a Greek discotheque. This was not an isolated occurrence. There was also Jade to consider, and perhaps she was the muse – a child comforting a lonely parent – for 'Fool To Cry', a kind of Stones 'You've Lost That Lovin' Feelin''. Featuring Mick emoting to his own electric-piano accompaniment, it was chosen to be the single from *Black And Blue*, an album born of the Mick Taylor/Ron Wood interregnum in 1975.

Yet, however tightly 'Fool To Cry' twisted the heartstrings, its composer seemed his old rampant self again by the time it clambered into the US and UK Top Tens in the middle of 1977 – at least, he implied as much over a meal with new-found friend Bryan Ferry. The two had much in common. Ferry, for example, was a fan of Jimmy Reed, paying his respects with an overhaul of 'Shame Shame Shame' on a recent EP. He and Jagger had similar tastes in women too, and it became painfully clear to Bryan that his fiancée, 21-year-old Jerry Hall – who had surfaced as one of Europe's top fashion models since her backpacking arrival in Paris in 1972 – was flattered by an instantly smitten Mick's subliminal – and not so subliminal – signals.

Blonde, leggy, pert-breasted, taller than Mick, and as comely (after a long-faced fashion) as his ex-wife in all but name, Hall's glamour was less calculated and her intellect less complicit than Bianca's. Hitherto, her Rolling Stone admirer had known Jerry principally as the mermaid-like figure on the sea-blue-tinted cover of Roxy Music's *Siren*, and for her low-cut dress and yee-hah exuberance during Ferry's mouth-organ solo on the video of his solo revival of Wilbert Harrison-via-Canned Heat's 'Let's Stick Together'.[5] During subsequent encounters without Bryan making three a crowd, Mick learned that she was one of five sisters, her close-knit family having been resident in Texas for more than three generations – to the extent that not only would a rich drawl and a passion for horse-riding betray her upbringing, but she could also boast some Cherokee blood.

As the oil economy skidded more rapidly into its recession, Texas had fallen back on its cradling of the Wild West. Dude ranches, rodeos, restored frontier forts, rattlesnake round-ups and establishments like Abilene's Old Betsy's Muzzle Loading Shop added to the mythologising of the recent cowboys-and-Injuns past represented by feature film, musical and TV series.

More likely career options than gunslinging and bronco-busting were to be found in, say, long-distance lorry-driving or clerkship, Jerry's father's and mother's respective professions. Just plain folks, they ensured that their children absorbed the innately decent 'sir' and 'ma'am' virtues of small-town America, smelling haughtiness and affectation a mile off. Guffawing and thigh-slapping, Jerry seemed the antithesis of Bianca – and the eclipsed Bryan Ferry's elegant stage persona – to tidy-minded scribes after tongues began to wag.

However, Mrs Hall was fond of Bryan and wasn't sure what to think of his face-saving claim that the romance had been over long before the persevering Jagger prised her beautiful daughter away. After three weeks in Morocco in November 1977, the lovers spent Christmas together in London and the New Year in Barbados and then Paris, where Jagger pushed aside a hovering photographer outside the Club Elysées Matignon. What made the spectacle different from similar ones was that the Frenchman didn't swallow the insult and skulk off. A martial-arts black belt, he seized Mick and flung him onto the pavement.

Glancing at the consequent tabloid shot of her husband, open-mouthed and grovelling, Bianca may have tittered with satisfaction. The journey to a formal dissolution of her dead marriage was protracted and rancorous, but concluded in London's stained-glass-windowed High Court on Guy Fawkes' Day, 1980, with her being awarded custody of Jade. She elected to continue bearing Jagger's name, but resisted selling her side of the story or allowing the nicotine-stained fingers of the press to jot down any profound comment about Mick beyond her valedictory 'I know people theorise that he thought it would be amusing to marry his twin, but actually Mick wanted to achieve the ultimate by making love to himself.'[6]

For those who collated recorded allusions about his personal life, there had been an avenue for enjoyable time-wasting on the follow-up to 'Fool To Cry', 1978's 'Miss You' – which was, in hard financial terms, bigger worldwide than anything else the Stones had ever released. A catchy harmonica riff was whistled by the milkman, while rhythmically the overall production was a concession to disco fever, then sashaying to its John Travolta zenith. Yet, when it blasted from John Lennon's car radio, he upped the volume further, remarking that Mick had got a great song from his divorce. Bianca may have agreed, but although he was reluctant to discuss its lyrical motive, Jagger explained that 'it's not really about a girl. To me, the feeling of longing is what the song is about.'[1]

'Miss You' was also the maiden release under a new distribution contract from February 1977 with EMI for six albums and publishing rights for everywhere except North America. Jagger expressing his views on the deal with, 'In this Jubilee Year, I think it is only fitting that we sign with a British company.'[1]

As well as marking the 25th anniversary of Elizabeth II's accession to the throne, 1977 was as much of a pop watershed year as 1963 had been. The punk thunderclap had resounded, and The Rolling Stones were being denounced by a fairweather music press as monied megastars forever in America and throwing a wobbler in a Hollywood Bowl dressing room on being supplied with *still* rather than *fizzy* mineral water. Musically, too, they and their kind were out of step with the inspired amateurism of rising acts as diverse as Television, Jonathan Richman And His Modern Lovers, The Ramones, The Sex Pistols, The Stranglers, Patti Smith, The UK Subs, Squeeze, The Police, Adam And The Ants, France's Les Thugs and, from Wales, Y Trwynau Coch. 'We're another generation,' scowled Joey of The Ramones. 'They're rich and living in another world altogether.'[7]

The wealth of some of pop's discredited Methuselahs wasn't entirely derived from record sales and concert fees. Herman of Herman's Hermits, for instance, had married into European aristocracy, while Phil May – once as much of a social pariah as Johnny Rotten of The Sex Pistols – had won the hand of a Stuart, and would be among those at Prince Charles' wedding to Lady Diana Spencer. 'I was invited by the Queen Mum,' shrugged May. 'My father-in-law had a grace-and-favour studio in the Palace. I'm probably 85th in line for the throne of Scotland.'

Mick Jagger was in with the Royal Family, too. During one of his many holidays, he'd become enchanted by the Caribbean island of Mustique. Scarcely more than a speck on the map, it was a hidden-away colony for British millionaires and blue-bloods. Princess Margaret had enjoyed its sunshine, sandy beaches and the shade of its coconut trees since the 1960s. She was to be a near-neighbour after Jagger applied for planning permission to build a house on a hill with a spellbinding view of a warm sea in which dolphins gambolled.

The Queen's prettier younger sister was more than just an acquaintance now. In 1976, she had been in the VIP enclosure at a Stones concert in Earl's Court, and was photographed afterwards congratulating Mick on his performance. On Mustique, he was a periodic guest on occasions that were a composite of candlelit regimental dinner and Polynesian *tamara* ('great meal'), which he attended along with other invitees from all walks of successful lives.

Smalltalk with Princess Margaret over coffee in a Caribbean twilight was another world away from punk-rock Britain, where The Sex Pistols' second single, 'God Save The Queen', was not reflective of monarchist fervour. Not a week went by without another hot young group ringing some changes. Somehow most of them were just like The Sex Pistols, with their ripped clothes, safety-pin earrings and guitars thrashed at speed to machine-gun drumming behind a ranting johnny-one-note, who'd given himself a self-denigrating *nom de théâtre* like 'Kenny Awful'.

Nonetheless, when in London, Mick had taken the trouble to experience for himself this street-level subculture that everyone was talking about. Johnny Rotten maintained that Jagger once peered into Sex, the Chelsea boutique that was the storm-centre of The Sex Pistols' operation. Pretending not to notice him, the principal carriers of the punk bacillus spoke in low voices and exchanged smirks. We hate your guts, you long-haired, complacent hippy git. Improved with age, the incident also had Rotten banging the door in Jagger's consternated face.

Down in the 100 Club, Mick listened to the Pistols' two-minute bursts of aural debris to appreciative Niagaras of spittle. At least it wasn't weak, this raw display of loathing, madness and retaliation – the very opposite of detached professional cool. He eyed Rotten and his cronies with a hint of apprehension, even admiration, then left without looking back.

There was food for thought too when he saw another show in the capital by Elvis Costello, Nick Lowe, Wreckless Eric and 30-something Ian Dury – crippled, pugnacious and described with vague accuracy by the *Daily Express*'s William Hickey as 'a sort of dirty old man of punk'[8] – as he spat out in 'oi-oi!' cockney his perspectives on London low life. For all the feigned disrespect towards anyone over 25, the disparate likes of Serge Gainsbourg, The Troggs, Gary Glitter and Bryan Ferry were admired too, and 1960s hitmaker Dave Berry was to be special guest of Adam And The Ants at the Strand Lyceum, where he swept aside a hostile audience as if they were matchsticks.

'Back In The USA' by that other Berry, Chuck, had been revived by Jonathan Richman, and 'Johnny B Goode' had been attempted during the Pistols' exploratory rehearsals. Meanwhile, back in the mainstream, Elvis Presley had scored in the Top Ten with Berry's 'The Promised Land', not long before news of his bathroom death in August 1977 raised a gleeful cheer in a dungeon-like hangout frequented by London punks. 'It's just too bad it couldn't have been Mick Jagger,'[6] was Sex Pistols Svengali Malcolm McLaren's[9] charitable comment.

Benignly, Jagger refused to bitch back at first, praising Squeeze, applauding The Police at the Bottom Line when he was next in New York, and seeming to align himself with punk's nihilism and trash aesthetic, assuring *Rolling Stone* that 'rock 'n' roll is a funny thing. There are two attitudes. One is like when Pete Townshend talks about it like a religion, and then there are others like me, who think it's really a lot of overblown nonsense. It's trash.'[10] He scorned the too-analytical form of pop journalism that intellectualises the unintellectual, turns perfume back into a rotten egg, and tells you what Jan Wenner thinks about *Black And Blue* and what Simon Frith thinks he means. 'Too many people are obsessed with pop,' acknowledged Jagger. 'The position of rock 'n' roll in our subculture has become far too important, especially in the delving for philosophical content.'[11]

These book-learnin' words aside, he might have started to convince any punk who didn't want to like him that he wasn't such a bad old bloke after all – except that, at the close of an *NME* interview in 1977, without being prompted, he launched into a vehement attack on The Stranglers, rubbishing their hard-man lyrics and aggressive antics, both on and off duty. He also laid into Patti Smith as 'a *poseur* of the worst kind, trying to be a street girl when she doesn't seem to be one'.[12] As for the Pistols, 'that bit about Johnny Rotten slamming the door on me is total fantasy. I don't even know where Sex is. There's a lot of clothes shops in the King's Road, and I've seen them all come and go. They all know I'm the only one who's got any money to spend on their crappy clothes. Though even I would draw the line on torn T-shirts.'[12]

Yet he wore one with 'DESTROY!' on the front for the Stones' only appearance in 1979, at a charity show in Toronto to fulfil what amounted to a community-service ruling imposed by a Canadian court on Keith Richards, guilty of drugs charges. Endless centuries of daily scrutiny of tapes of two concerts undertaken during the 1977 week of Keith's arrest had revealed to Mick that there were only so many fantastic mixes of 'Around And Around' or 'Little Red Rooster' that could be endured in one session. When the resulting album, *Love You Live* – a title at deliberately doe-eyed odds with punk – was mastered, he sighed that 'nine months of listening to The Rolling Stones isn't my idea of heaven'.[6]

Attending to *Love You Live*'s exploitation too, he gave his blessing to a press kit containing a pair of rubber lips, visualising perhaps office jokers putting them on and doing a Jagger impression. Condoning such mockery of yourself was cheap and shallow, but necessary.

Pop music, eh? Who needed it? It was becoming something of a run-of-the-mill job, one that he'd been doing for years. For every creative act, there was an infinity of tedious mechanical processes. Sometimes, he couldn't wait for knocking-off time. 'My whole life isn't rock 'n' roll,' he elucidated while weathering the punk storm. 'It's an absurd idea that it should be, but it's no more than anybody's whole life should revolve around working in Woolworth's'.[13]

15 Shoot Me, Baby

'I feel that I can go on singing live for a long time, although obviously I can't do the high-energy stuff for ever – but while I still can, I might as well carry on.'

– *Mick Jagger*[1]

Bob Marley's interventions in West Indian politics had won him both an assassination attempt and a United Nations Third World Peace Medal that recognised efforts symbolised by him cajoling Jamaica's Prime Minister and, looking like thunder, its Opposition leader to shake hands during Bob and his Wailers' 'One Love' finale at a Peace Concert in Kingston's National Stadium on 22 April 1978. Mick Jagger was present but not performing there, and three months later at a Marley bash in Los Angeles – with Jade and Jerry in tow – on the evening before the closing show – at Anaheim Stadium along the coast – of the first Stones tour of the USA since 1975.

Not able to rely so much on youthful metabolism as general physical maintenance, Mick had trained for the expedition as a boxer would for a world-title fight, except that, rather than sparring or pounding a punchbag, he was rowing, cycling, weightlifting, running and – since the altercation with the Parisian photographer – practising karate, as well as performing the sit-ups, press-ups and similar exercises that had been his habit since childhood. 'When you get to my age, you really have to work at staying young,' he conceded. 'Once I led the typical dissipated life of a rock star, full of drugs and booze and chaos, but these days my health is my most treasured possession. When I'm on tour, I never touch hard liquor, and I try to get as much sleep as I possibly can.'[2]

From a civic centre in Florida to Anaheim six weeks later, he went the distance without difficulty night after night, entertaining 80,000 – the largest ever indoor audience – at the New Orleans Superdrome on 13 July. This date alone grossed more than a million greenbacks in ticket sales, on top of takings on the plethoric merchandising that mopped up ticket-buyers' spare change.

The only major upset was a riot somewhere in New York State when demands for an encore weren't met. More insidious were mitherings about degradation and political incorrectness from an organisation called Women Against Violence Against Women over *Some Girls*, the album from which 'Miss You' had been taken. Just as there'd been disquiet about a Hollywood billboard of a bruised and bound woman to publicise 1976's *Black And Blue*, the latest effort's title track, with its lyrical generalisations, based on Jagger's apparent experience, about the sexual predilections of particular racial types of female, raised hackles. In parenthesis, 'Some Girls' also in-joked about Bob Dylan's recent divorce – for which he was attempting to soften the blow of the resulting alimony with a lucrative and extensive world tour.

Marianne Faithfull was back before the footlights, too. Her comeback had gained ground in 1974, when, clad in a cross between a nun's habit and buttock-revealing mini-dress, she'd sung with David Bowie – himself a sartorial vision in stiletto heels and black fishnet – on *Midnight Special*, a TV extravaganza from the Marquee, networked in the States.

Her voice proved to be shorn of its former mezzo-soprano purity when, reunited with Andrew Loog Oldham as producer, she recorded Waylon Jennings' 'Dreaming My Dreams', a water-testing single that was a hit in Eire if nowhere else. Next, she visited the UK Top 50 for the first time in 12 years with 1979's 'The Ballad Of Lucy Jordan'. Grippingly and chain-smokingly rough, the re-emerged Marianne took several steps further forward – in guts, if not marketability – with that same year's *Broken English*, an album that was as much a fixture in student halls of residence as the poster of Che Guevara had been years earlier. She was soon to be ploughing the same lived-in furrows as Marlene Dietrich, Billie Holiday and Lotte Lenya with such as wartime 'Gloomy Sunday' – perhaps the most depressing song of the past century[3] – and a world-weary retread of 'As Tears Go By'.

Marianne had also been sounded out for a role in *The Great Rock 'n' Roll Swindle* – a kind of subjective *Hard Day's Night* – for a Sex Pistols in disarray as the result of a *casus belli* between Rotten and McLaren. Soon, punk was but a memory for the man in the street, although tracks like 'Lies' on the Stones' *Some Girls* had paid heed to it, as much as items like their own frantic 'She Said Yeah' and – also from 1965 – The Pretty Things' 'Honey I Need' had anticipated it.

Punk attitude seemed to have rubbed off on a prattle of London's media gentlefolk flown over to review the Stones at the New York Palladium. 'They were brought over here to see us,' sniffed a disgusted Jagger, 'and all they wanted to do was get drunk. They are trash. I'd never live in England again, not when people like that are living there.'[4]

As if in acknowledgement, details of Cheyne Walk were with an estate agent and Jagger was house-hunting in central France, selecting eventually a Loire Valley château that he would decorate with Picassos, Renoirs and Van Goghs. While it offered both rustic calm and close proximity to Paris, Jagger's principal residence in the early 1980s was a second-floor Manhattan apartment overlooking Central Park[5] – and not far from the snooty Dakota block, where John Lennon had metamorphosed into Yoko Ono's reclusive 'househusband', providing their only child, Sean, with more paternal attention than most.

As Paul McCartney had been turned away from the door via intercom, what chance did Jagger have of chewing the fat with

Lennon? Without much hope, he gave a note to the Dakota doorman, but he was still waiting for a reply on 8 December 1980, when John was gunned down by a nutcase named Mark David Chapman. Accosted for comment outside a Parisian studio, Mick, nearly at a loss for words, was not ready 'to make a casual remark right now at such an awful moment for his family'.[6]

John's murder summoned fears of a copycat killing, especially as the homicidal Chapman had been photographed stalking Dylan, too. 'John's shooting definitely scared all of us – me, Paul and Ringo,' admitted George Harrison. 'When a fan recognises me and rushes over, it definitely makes me nervous.'[7] George's trepidation would be justified when a paranoid schizophrenic – from Liverpool, of all places – stabbed him in his own home two decades later.

For the Stones – the others most likely to be targeted – the perturbing psychological repercussions of Lennon's slaying would be compounded when, in the queue outside Seattle's Kingdome on the next tour, a deranged woman attracted the attention of patrolling police by brandishing a revolver and spluttering about how she was going to worm her way to within point-blank range of Jagger.

Lennon's passing was also both an end and a beginning, simultaneously the most public last gasp and the ricochet of a starting pistol for a qualified rebirth of the Swinging '60s. Witness Bob Hite's fatal heart attack the following April, which, rather than presenting an opportune moment for disbanding Canned Heat, was regarded as regrettable but not disastrous. Thus the droning rhythm synonymous with the group continued to underpin old crowd-pleasers as records became less important than earnings on the road. Similarly, money would be among chief incentives for a reassembly of the original Animals for a 1983 global tour that fixed unashamedly on their back catalogue – although, for form's sake, they gave audiences a couple of tracks from a reunion album on sale in the foyer on the way out.

That the transmission of one of The Animals' concerts on prime-time television proved a worthwhile exercise was a further indication that the nostalgia orbit was no longer such a netherworld. No 1960s relic grew old there. Each was still a legendary hero who would offend none by refusing to autograph a dog-eared EP cover depicting him with most of his hair still on his head, even if some acts weren't the full shilling – Gerry and a too-youthful Pacemakers, say, a Herman's Hermits *sans* Herman or Rick Huxley's replacement of The Barron Knights' ailing leader.

Yet, while The Blues Band – formed by ex-Manfred Menn in 1979 – leaned heavily on the Mann portfolio, and, four years later, a Yardbirds containing three original members played their ancient hits at the Marquee during the club's anniversary celebrations, The Pretty Things – with a re-enlisted Dick Taylor – took stock after a three-year layoff and decided not to look forward to the days gone by. As astute a businessman as Jagger, in his way, Phil May's negotiations with Warner Brothers had yielded a surprisingly fat advance for a new album, 'because Karen Berg, head of A&R, liked what we'd done so far for what became *Crosstalk*', but she 'left the firm, and we were to be marketed by a whole new set of people'. As the new album was loaded into delivery vans, the situation was aggravated further by an *exposé* of Warner's on the TV current-affairs programme *World In Action* revealing 'all the backhanders, bottles of Scotch, cocaine and whatever else was needed to rig the charts', wailed viewer Dick Taylor.

This crestfallen headway coincided with May's re-entry into Jagger's social circle, where, so it was reported, Mick owned up to copying Phil's onstage gyrations – and wasn't the 'Honey I Need' lurch later grafted onto the Stones' go at 'Chantilly Lace' for 1982's global barnstormer?

Although Jagger – like May – could also count members of the royal family among his chums, he and three ex-Beatles had doled out impromptu and ragged cabaret on a makeshift stage, deep in the Surrey countryside, at Eric Clapton's star-studded wedding reception in 1979. He was also amenable to jamming with Muddy Waters in a Chicago club on two occasions at the turn of the decade, the latter of which was filmed and the footage stored in the Stones' archives. A clip would be incorporated into 1989's *25 x 5*, a self-made documentary subtitled *The Continuing Adventures Of The Rolling Stones* – contradicting Jagger's punk-era ennui and a later statement to a tabloid journalist that 'the band has done what it set out to do; it will disintegrate very slowly'.[8] The Stones, it seemed, were still belligerently alive in spite of assorted earlier schisms that had all but torn them apart.

In 1980, however, Jagger had been weighing up the cash benefits of pop against his self-picture as a musician. 'How long do you want to be in rock 'n' roll?' a *Melody Maker* newshound had enquired. Mick's face – then temporarily bearded to the cheekbones – pinched in thought before he replied a deliberated, 'I dunno. Maybe forever?'[9] Yet, later that same month, he'd reckon that 'rock 'n' roll has no future. It's only recycled past.'[10]

Creatively, the Stones were running out of steam. Though *Emotional Rescue* – the album they'd been finishing when Lennon was shot – had swept with mathematical precision to the top in Britain and the US, it conveyed a sense of marking time. 'There's hardly a melody here you haven't heard from the Stones before,' affirmed *Rolling Stone*. 'This word-perfect, classic-sounding, spiritless record is a message from the grave. I'm afraid that people won't be calling them survivors much longer.'[10] Nevertheless, adoration would be for life – or, at least, years a-dwindling – for the faithful, but after *Emotional Rescue* many ceased buying Stones albums to complete the set like Buffalo Bill annuals.

Mick spoke about downing tools as a Stone to intimates such as David Bowie. An eavesdropper spread the tale that he was intending to devote himself solely to films, starting with a remake of the 1959 farce *Some Like It Hot*, with himself assuming the Jack Lemmon part and Bowie that of Tony Curtis, and both dressing up as ladies. Another dismissed proposal was acting in and producing a celluloid adaptation of the Gore Vidal play *Kalki*.

Jagger's procrastinations appeared to be over when he brushed up his *Ned Kelly* brogue for a role as an eccentric Irishman attempting to establish an opera house in the Peruvian outback in *Fitzcarraldo*, which vied with 1975's *The Enigma Of Kasper Hauser* as the best-known film by German director Werner Herzog. In general circulation by 1983, *Fitzcarraldo* was praised by critics, although Jagger's connection with it had dissipated within weeks of him arriving on location in Iquitos, 3,000 miles from the Amazon delta across jagged peaks, sun-scorched desert and jungle. So remote was the setting that tropical disease was a way of life (and death), the cast were billeted in mosquito-ridden mud huts, and loincloth-clad natives – descendants of headhunters – glowered at, belaboured and stopped just short of openly assaulting the foreign intruders.

Initially, Mick mucked in, helping the crew lug and set up equipment while muttering his lines over and over again. One February day, however, he felt so sick and miserable that he dragged himself to the nearest airport and slipped smoothly into the skies and out of an intolerable situation.

Herzog chose to try again in May, but by then his errant star was in the throes of readying himself for another album-tour-album sandwich. Come September, the new LP, entitled *Tattoo You*, plus its 'Start Me Up' 45 – destined to be *Rolling Stone*'s Single Of The Year – had been positioned in their respective charts, and every date of the US leg had sold out.

For what was a mammoth undertaking these days, preparation was costly, even when offset by corporate sponsorship.[11] In 1962, the back room of a pub had sufficed, but now the Stones and an entourage of 30 were renting a huge barn converted into rehearsal rooms, on an olde-worlde hill farm in rural Massachusetts. It was necessary to hog the entire complex so that other musicians couldn't book time and disturb their sleep in daylight hours prior to gone-midnight rambles down memory lane as far back as 'Come On' – from which the world at large would be spared, but which could be perceived miles across open countryside from where the Stones had lost themselves in music 'til dawn.

At times, it gave the impression that it could fall to bits at any given moment, although there were passages as squeaky-clean and as preordained as a Broadway musical, such as Jagger's choreographed head turning abruptly in Richards' direction for the 'partner in crime' line in 'Tumbling Dice'.

As was now customary, Mick had a hand in the set design, which centred on a hydraulically operated revolving stage that turned with a slowness more majestic than that at the London Palladium, invoking mid-song cheers whenever the Stones hove into full-frontal view of particular sections of the audience. More astounding was a cherry-picker bearing Mick (and its glumly seated operator), darting fitfully in and out of the crowd – just out of reach – for the fixed 'Satisfaction' encore.

Mick's litmus test of the spectacular's intrinsic quality was the reaction of those he knew wouldn't necessarily want to like it. Chatting amicably enough to Bianca after Madison Square Garden on 15 November, he believed her when, with eyes alight with rueful pride in him, she exclaimed, 'It was superb! The Stones seem to get better as the years go on.'[4]

Yet not a day went by without some twit from the media imagining that he was the first to come up with the headline, COULD THIS BE THE LAST TIME?! No, it wouldn't, parried Jagger, albeit while estimating that 'Within three or four years, I won't be able to do what I do now on stage any more.'[4]

He remained a role model to younger rock vocalists, most conspicuously, lookalike Steve Tyler of once-and-future US chart contenders Aerosmith, for whom Jagger's still-acrobatic stage craft was received wisdom. Many rungs below Aerosmith, countless other groups of the same stripe would be heaving amplifiers into vans as the Stones jetted overhead, miles above towns that hadn't been built when they'd crossed the United States almost as a freak show in 1964.

When the 1982 juggernaut invaded Britain, the past hit the ground running via a short-notice appearance on the low stage within the time-hallowed walls of the 400-capacity 100 Club. The word had got around within hours, and fire regulations were flouted as the crush in the belly of the club seeped up the stairs and onto Oxford Street, where some over-excited souls pressed their ears to the dirty pavement, straining to catch the faintest leakage from down below.

16 I Ain't Got You

> 'I couldn't make a total Rolling Stones album without Keith.
> I could make another kind of album of course…'
>
> – *Mick Jagger*[1]

Jagger told *Woman's World* that he didn't intend to marry again. Once was quite enough, thank you. How was Jerry expected to take this and disclosures like it? More insidiously, a man as busy as Mick was apt to be an inattentive boyfriend. He didn't seem to be trying all that hard any more – and, after seeing too many photographs in the newspaper of him with socialites, models and further gold diggers who materialised like vultures to see and be seen with him, there proved to be a limit to Jerry's loyalty and affection after five years. Her frank nature would not permit her to remain silent about his emotional indolence. With the same questions coming up again and again, she stopped groping for reasons that would explain and excuse his conduct, and while he was away on 1982's European tour, she decided she'd had enough.

That there was an exciting development in the ongoing Rolling Stones soap opera became evident to fans via the dictum that the most pig-ugly bloke has to be the series' sex symbol and pull the tastiest birds. Though the distinguished British racehorse-owner and -breeder Robert Sangster wasn't actually a bad-looking fellow after a paunchy fashion, he was short-haired, sports-jacketed, cavalry-twilled, trilby-hatted and very middle-aged. Having inherited millions from his tycoon father, he'd established a virtual monopoly on victories in principal races throughout Britain and

France through employment of jockeys like the fêted Lester Piggott, as well as the means to acquire any thoroughbred that took his fancy. When he assured friends, 'There's nobody on Earth who can outbid me when I've set my mind on buying a horse,'[2] none of them doubted him for a second.

Other of Sangster's pursuits included golf and women. He was no Arnold Palmer, but the reek of money that spread from him like cigar smoke was among factors that ensured more romantic conquests than most.

In June 1982, he captured Jerry Hall's heart at Royal Ascot, perhaps the most important meet on the equine sports calendar. Their eyes met, he beamed his fleshy smile and contact was established. Then rubbing her chin over the purchase of a stud farm in Texas, had Jerry ever enjoyed a more interesting conversation?

Within months, it was rumoured that she and Robert were about to name the day; the *Daily Mail* making waves with Jerry's accusations of Jagger's abusive behaviour, and the *Los Angeles Times* hurling a stone at his retreating back by quoting her venomous 'Where could I go after Mick? Robert could buy him out ten times over.'[3]

You always hurt the one you love, and if her betrothal had any foundation in fact, it was recognised as a registered protest rather than boat-burning by Mick, who had won Jerry back in time for Christmas on Mustique, but on the understanding that marriage – however far into the future – was an eventuality rather than a remote possibility.

A less personal upheaval was to take place now that EMI and Atlantic's time was up. Representatives from every major company put forward their bids. 'It amused Mick to see so many record executives chasing him around the world,' noted CBS's Walter Yetnikoff. 'He was a skilled negotiator who never lost sight of his advantage as a pop icon.'[4]

He seemed most enticed by CBS, who dangled the carrot of solo albums as well as the biggest advance ever proffered for a pop group. Yet, battle-hardened by the industry, he didn't show too much eagerness, spoke in riddles and, cried Yetnikoff, 'kept me running for a year. Meetings in Europe, New York, California – the challenge of Jagger's swagger and sinewy ways took all I had. One of my first had been in a swanky Parisian restaurant, ordering wine that cost more than the GNP of certain countries. We were both bombed – or at least I was. You could never tell with Mick. He liked to give the impression of inebriation while retaining control.

'The highly complex contract was already drafted. It required a dozen lawyers and involved a Dutch Antilles holding company. After months of haggling, all we needed were signatures. That's when Mick balked.'[4]

With the approbation of Keith Richards, Jagger's irresolution was chiefly over a clause concerning whether the Stones or CBS should select each album's two singles. Purportedly, Jagger caved in after a frightful table-banging quarrel with Yetnikoff that you could hear all over the same French diner in which the drawn-out discussions had started.

More often than not an album's most trite cut, a single was a fiddly little thing anyway, more likely to be a loss-leader than an unmistakable worldwide smash nowadays. No matter how they were packaged – 12-inch club mix or polkadot vinyl – 45s were becoming no more than radio-playlist inducements to shell out for LPs – unless you were Gary Glitter, for whom they were avenues for publicising albumless tours as the *kitsch* darling of the college circuit, the consequence of his rebirth as a British pop treasure, assured of well-paid work for as long as he could stand. Glitter had just had a minor windfall with a retread of a Crystals hit from 1963, but not as minor as the Stones' rehash of their 1964 cover of trusty old 'Time Is On My Side', taken from the 1982 in-concert album *Still Life*.

Exhuming old songs was becoming a common practice for others, too. The Pretty Things had been responsible for an audacious crack at 'Eve Of Destruction' – with its 1965 topical verses unrevised – as Chris Farlowe would be for a re-run of Long John Baldry's 1967 Number One, 'Let The Heartaches Begin', while the title theme for Chris Jagger's proposed 'swingtime musical' – 1930s standard 'It Ain't What You Do, It's The Way That You Do It' – had been a 1982 chart strike for The Fun Boy Three, sprung from a ska revival in the late 1970s.

Next up for the Stones, however, would be an original, 1983's 'Undercover Of The Night', with a Jagger libretto about *Nacht und Nebel* raids that began the process of the vapourising of political dissidents in repressive South America republics. A dramatic video with himself as the victim was screened during an interview on *The Tube* – a Channel 4 pop showcase intended to be a *Ready Steady Go de ses jours* – although the cameras panned away from a particularly bloodstained sequence to Mick, whose staged wincing turned a promotional tool that might have passed without comment into a mild *cause célèbre*.

'Undercover Of The Night', therefore, commenced a scramble to the brink of the Top Ten. From the same *Undercover* album, however, 'One Hit (To The Body)' was the first to miss the domestic Top 50 completely, and it struggled in the US Top 40, too. A resurrection of 'Harlem Shuffle' – a turntable hit on pirate radio in the mid-1960s for New York-based soul duo Bob and Earl – turned out to be the last unarguable smash on both sides of the ocean for a future invested with a suspicion that the Stones were in a slow but sure decline. CBS derived what gain it could from the situation, but the group's previous handlers considered themselves lucky to have milked the Stones when they did.

The scum of internal disharmony was surfacing, too, and it boiled down to Mick and Keith, now the group's self-appointed record producers. The lead singer did not subscribe to the maxim that, if a thing's worth doing, it's worth doing pedantically, while the guitarist's constant retakes and overdubbing of minor fills were starting to pall. Nonetheless, Mick's own fastidiousness in other creative areas was just as irritating. 'If we're doing a video, it's never right,' complained Charlie Watts. 'He can never just leave it alone. He has to go and spend another £4,000.'[5] Yet Watts sympathised with Jagger when Richards chose to go on a holiday in Jamaica in the middle of the New York mixing sessions for *Undercover*.

Fanning dull embers, nonetheless, Keith was to steer the Stones towards 1986's relatively uncluttered *Dirty Work*, but brisk finesse and riding roughshod over gratuitous frills could not dispel a flagrant spirit of malcontented shiftlessness. Of late, Bill had been talking with increasing frequency of his long-mooted plan to quit the group, and was surrendering more and more of the bass-playing chores to Keith, who was muttering his exasperation about the sessions' depressing similarity to those for *Exile On Main Street*. 'Mick was there so infrequently for *Dirty Work*,' Richards would sigh in retrospect. 'It was just Charlie, Ronnie and me trying to make a Stones record. It was very unprofessional of Mick.'[6]

Yet, other than the most subtle sleights of social judo, there'd been no outright animosity or any sense that Bill, Charlie and Ron were waiting for either Mick or Keith to marshall his words and dare a speech that he'd been agonising over for months. 'It's a very English relationship, where not a lot is said,'[7] Jagger would discern with the candour of greater age.

Nevertheless, the wheels of the Stones' universe were no longer as interlocking as they had been, because of the difficulties of trying to usher the intimacy of Mick and Keith's life-defining adolescent friendship into adult life. As well as the polarisation of inner natures and desires that advancing years engender, this may be summarised perhaps by the hookline of 'Wedding Bells', a 1929 opus rearranged for Gene Vincent almost three decades later: 'Those wedding bells are breaking up that old gang of mine.'

To Keith, Jerry wasn't quite the *bête noire* that Bianca had been, and Mick had been best man when Keith had married in 1983. Even so, 'settling down' and – as exemplified by nappy-changing Lennon's terse and electronically relayed words to McCartney –

the coming of children can push friendships into the background, often creating a void as piquant as a bereavement.

Mick's first child with Jerry had come to consciousness in New York's Lennox Hill Hospital on 2 March 1984 – and Shirley Watts, Charlie's wife, was godmother when Elizabeth Scarlett was christened in London. Other than Charlie, no other Stone was there, just as Keith had been the only one present at Mick's registry-office wedding to Bianca.

While Watts didn't feel qualified to unravel the tangled web of Jagger and Richards' personal bond, he attributed 'a combination of Keith's spirit and Mick's drive' as the key to the Stones' longevity: 'You could say Keith brings emotion and Mick brings direction. Mick on his own would have lost the way years ago if he hadn't Keith to bounce off – and vice-versa, because without Mick pushing, there's no way we would have been able to do it for this long.'[5]

Jagger himself confessed, 'It makes for a very complicated relationship. I still don't really pretend to understand it.'[8] However, he could understand perfectly why Bill didn't want to be a Rolling Stone unto the grave. He and the bass guitarist were drifting apart, anyway. 'Seven or eight years ago, I could talk with Mick about books, films and intelligent things,' mourned Wyman, 'but now I just talk to him in asides.'[9] More business associates than mates these days, the two had, nevertheless, collaborated on a video for 1984's *Rewind*, a compilation of the EMI years.

The mist of closure shrouding the Stones thickened as, between *Undercover* and *Dirty Work*, Mick had been allocated several weeks at pricey Compass Point Studios in the Bahamas for his first solo LP, an undertaking guaranteed to generate more media interest than, say, 1976's *Stone Alone*, Bill's second in his own right; Ron Wood's *Gimme Some Neck* (his third); or Keith's potshot at the singles chart with Chuck Berry's 'Run Rudolph Run' in 1979. Even Charlie's extramural jazz combos had released records.

However, it wasn't possible to pour oil over the present troubled waters by insisting that Mick's maiden offering would Enrich the

Group as a Whole, any more than another cliché – Musical Differences – would ring true then if the break-up of the Stones had been announced formally. The split wasn't decisive enough for that. Even so, Keith had, apparently, opened a 'what if' dialogue with Roger Daltrey. After all, The Hollies had survived the departure of lead singer Allan Clarke, just as Manfred Mann had gone on without the equally charismatic Paul Jones.

Had it come to it, Daltrey might have jumped at the chance, as The Who weren't much of a group any more, either. This had been painfully obvious to Jagger when he walked in on a backstage tongue-lashing that seemed bereft of any underlying affection: 'I learned a lesson from The Who being on the road when they were not getting on. It embarrassed me and made me feel sad, and I don't want to see The Rolling Stones like that. When you're not getting on, don't push it in public. I don't want to stand still and wait for the problems to go away, for everyone to come around and be in the right mood. I love the Stones, but it cannot be, at my age, the only thing in my life.'[9]

The first overt indication of this was Jagger's accepting an invitation to duet with Michael Jackson on 'State Of Shock', the hit single from 1984's *Victory* by the former Tamla Motown child star and his elder brothers.

Teaming up with another artist often proved a viable strategy during the 1980s. Alliances on 45 by Jackson and Paul McCartney, McCartney and Stevie Wonder, Queen and David Bowie, Bowie and Bing Crosby(!), gnarled Joe Cocker and fresh-faced Jennifer Warnes, Don Everly and Cliff Richard, Cliff Richard and Van Morrison, and Gene Pitney and crypto-punk vocalist Marc Almond had all yielded chartbusting bonanzas.

So did a resuscitation of Martha And The Vandellas' 'Dancing In The Street' by Bowie and Jagger, although it earned neither of them a penny, issued as it was as a fundraiser for Live Aid. Created in eight hours, a video of Mick and David doing their bit was screened prior to Jagger's appearance on the programme in person on 13 July 1985 – 20 years to the day after the Stones were at Number One in the US with 'Satisfaction' – at Philadelphia's JFK Stadium, despite protestations that, 'I don't believe in being a charity queen, to make the likely rounds, turning up at charity balls and dinners, wearing my diamonds.'[10]

Backed by local lads Hall And Oates and their band,[11] Mick's first ever show without the Stones embraced 'Miss You' and a 'State Of Shock' that segued into 'It's Only Rock 'n' Roll', a duet with Tina Turner that reached boiling point with him ripping off her skirt – just as the male members had unclad the female half of Bucks Fizz during 1981's Eurovision Song Contest, which Mick knew none of the Yanks would have seen.

Jagger also inserted a couple of numbers from *She's The Boss*, the long-awaited solo album that, still in record shop windows months after it was shipped out in March, had spawned 'Just Another Night', which reached the Top 30 in Britain while achieving a high of Number Ten in the States. A second *She's The Boss* single, 'Lucky In Love', was lingering still in the Hot 100.

We never see the man. We see only his art. I mean this most sincerely, friends. So how could we ever know if Jagger at Live Aid was motivated by a simple desire to help the starving – to which end he also recorded a spoken link on the associated video compilation – or seizing an unforeseeable but welcome opportunity to trumpet *She's The Boss*?

It wasn't entirely necessary, but, if it was deliberate, he'd allowed the album the best possible chance by bolstering the credits with credible and negotiable names, among them Pete Townshend of The Who, jazz-rock behemoths Herbie Hancock and Jan Hammer, trend-setting producer Nile Rodgers and Carlos Alomar, who supplied music for two Jagger lyrics and who, like Keith Richards, had became known principally as a rhythm guitarist. Alomar's apprenticeship in James Brown's Famous Flames and his tenure in the house band at the Sigma Sound complex – from which emanated Philadelphia's feathery soul style in the 1970s – had led an irregular Sigma client, David Bowie, to retain Alomar as a full-time accompanist and sometime bandleader on tour and on disc.

While Carlos wasn't heard on *She's The Boss*, the influence of his urgent fretboard precision and his terse *ostinati*-picking pervaded such as 'Lucky In Love', 'Turn The Girl Loose' and lesser instances of Mick slipping into a James Brown-esque groove. Overall, however, it was what you might have imagined the Stones sounding like if Jeff Beck had filled, afterall, the post left vacant by Mick Taylor in 1974. Loud and clear on 'Lonely At The Top' (once earmarked for *Tattoo You*), 'Running Out Of Luck' (on finger-style acoustic six-string), 'Lucky In Love' and three more of the LP's nine tracks, Beck's solos and passage-work were as indelible a signature as Jagger's baritone.

Dubbed 'the Paganini of the guitar' by no less than Malcolm McLaren,[12] Beck kept his devotees guessing what he'd be up to next as a verification of the merits of sweating over something new, while more famous contemporaries – like his Yardbirds predecessor Eric Clapton – turned out increasingly more ordinary albums. 'I just like to condition my audience to be ready for anything, rather than turn their noses up because I've done a weird album,'[13] averred Jeff.

If, in Mick's opinion, 'very patient, and very hard-working',[13] the talented Jeff could also be as sullenly temperamental as Keith Richards. One source of his huffs was a tendency not to 'get' jokes, storming out of Compass Point Studios when an impish Mick pretended to direct an engineer to erase a particularly startling *She's The Boss* solo.[14]

A pot calling a kettle black, Beck found Jagger 'a very moody guy. He would strum chords for about three hours to get into the mood. By that time, I was tired, and he wouldn't show any signs of appreciation or pleasure at what you were doing. "Oh yeah, that was all right. Let's call it a day." You go home and you feel dejected. It was difficult.'[13]

Both in between sessions and prior to flying to the Bahamas, Mick crafted his lyrics as carefully as a cementer would a mosaic, sometimes picking the brain of brother Chris. These covered a broad range of ideas, from the Hollywood hopeful rapidly saddened by brush-offs and unreturned calls in 'Lonely At The Top' to the frustrated smokescreening of an affair in 'Half A Loaf' to the pleading despair and submissiveness of 'Hard Woman' and the title song. Elsewhere, self-regret about a cash-haemorrhaging addiction to gambling is mitigated by success with the ladies in harmonica-tinged 'Lucky In Love', while 'Running Out Of Luck' seems to be riven with intimations about division of property with a former lover.

The words were printed on the inner sleeve of a package that garnered mixed reviews. The most favourable – headlined 'HE'S THE BOSS!' – was from *Melody Maker*, but the bulk of the album's 2 million sales were overseas. Every silver lining has a cloud, however, and a multi-million dollar suit for plagiarism – because reggae executant Patrick Alley detected too great a similarity between 'Just Another Night' and his own 1982 opus of the same title – was to haunt Jagger until May 1988, when it was thrown out of a New York court – though not before he delighted the public gallery by singing a few bars to demonstrate his counsel's argument.

Thus the century's final decade loomed, with Mick Jagger as – predictably – the most engaging and commercially operative Rolling Stone, and yet seemingly under no economic or artistic pressure ever to tread the boards with the group again. He gave an outward impression, too, of a person completely in command of his faculties, an affluent family man in perfect health with only the most transient worries. Yet, though distanced from him now, Keith Richards perceived that his old pal was 'not living a happy life. Ninety-nine per cent of the male population of the Western world – and beyond – would give a limb to be him, but he's not happy being Mick Jagger.'[9]

17 You're Gonna Need My Help

'People want you to be like you were in 1969, because otherwise their youth goes with you. It's very selfish, but it's understandable.'

– Mick Jagger[1]

In 1986, Little Richard was cast as a street-corner evangelist in the US cops-and-robbers vehicle *Miami Vice*, and Jerry Hall's old *beau* Bryan Ferry had a one-episode cameo in a French equivalent of *Crossroads*, the long-running ITV series, set in a hotel. By the conventions of pop hierarchy, it was almost a matter of course that a role in *Dallas* – then a prime-time US soap almost beyond parody – was dangled in front of Mick, and, after he turned it down, Ringo Starr.

Partly because she was Jagger's 'constant companion', Hall herself was wooed by theatre, TV and film directors, just as Bianca had been. With Mick's encouragement, she took on the female lead in the comedy-drama *Bus Stop*, which opened at the Montclair Stage College Theater in New Jersey on 26 July 1988. Improvising around her own personality and background, she was as powerful as Marilyn Monroe had been in the 1956 screen version as 'Cherie', a rodeo-town bar-room entertainer who marries a naive backwoodsman. Two years later, the production was to transfer successfully to London's West End, following an out-of-town tryout at the Palace Theatre, Watford.

Partly because she was Jagger's constant companion, too, Jerry had been central figure in an incident in a Barbados customs area that had concluded with her detention in a police cell after an arrest because a unlabelled parcel containing marijuana and posted to the airport's main desk was assumed to be hers. Bailed, she was obliged to wait one nerve-jangling month for a 'not guilty' verdict.

This was the only major hiccough in an otherwise untroubled existence then. Elizabeth Scarlett now had a brother, James Leroy Augustine, born on 28 August 1985. Both were to be the only family members in attendance at their parents' wedding on 21 November 1990 in Bali by a Hindu holy man. The ceremony lasted hours, and although Hinduism is the most tolerant and gentle of faiths, advocating kindness to animals among other qualities, the ritual allegedly embraced the sacrifice of a small bird.

Balancing motherhood, marriage and career, Jerry had, when pregnant with James, co-hosted *Andy Warhol's Fifteen Minutes*, an MTV pilot hosted by a man not long for this world who had metamorphosed into a bland media personality with an intriguing past. Maybe that was almost the point, as was the eventual use of his Velvet Underground's 'Venus In Furs' in all its sado-masochistic glory to soundtrack an ITV commercial. Warhol had remained a mutual friend of both Jerry and Bianca, though each had given the other a wide berth when they'd attended unwittingly the same International AIDS Day concert at Wembley Arena on 1986's April Fool's Day.

The first Mrs Jagger's concern too about iniquities against the innocent in South and Central America was more hands-on than merely composing a hit song about them. Her shocked inspection of a United Nations refugee camp was exacerbated when she also witnessed an armed death squad from El Salvador barging in and, without a by-your-leave, rounding up some 40 incumbents with whom they had grievances. It was Bianca's harrying of officialdom that prevented an otherwise certain bloodbath.

Just as fiercely prosecuted two decades later, Bianca's campaigns for human rights – in Palestine, Bosnia, Serbia and Zambia, too – and her pragmatic support of Greenpeace, Friends Of The Earth and like causes were recognised in the form of awards from bodies such as the American Civil Liberties Union, and executive positions in the Leadership Council for Amnesty International, USA, and the Advisory Committee for Human Rights.

Another who'd borne a child by Mick Jagger would also give herself to good works, chiefly by running a writers' workshop for young offenders in Dublin's Mountjoy Prison. Marsha Hunt's showbusiness enterprises, however, had been multi-faceted since the release of 'The Beast Day'. She hosted her own Capital Radio chat show and, since 1982, had been a member of the National Theatre Company for three years. As both a singer and a straight actor, she featured subsequently in all manner of motion-picture, television and stage productions.

One evening backstage in a West End theatre, Hunt's path had crossed that of Marianne Faithfull, who had been readying herself to enter stage left. As a singer, Marianne had been typecast as a cabaret-performing *femme fatale*, visiting every avenue of her musical career on *Blazing Away*, a 1990 concert album recorded at a New York cathedral. A later album, *The Seven Deadly Sins*, focused on her – and the Vienna Radio Symphony Orchestra's – interpretation of the 1933 ballet-*cum*-song cycle that marked Kurt Weill and Marxist playwright Bertold Brecht's final collaboration – with Marianne as a central character more worldly than Brecht and Weill may have envisaged, mainly through the pitching of the part a necessary octave lower than in the original arrangement to accommodate a husky passion.

In 1996, Weill's name also surfaced regularly on Marianne's *20th Century Blues* – subtitled 'An Evening In The Weimar Republic' – replete with genre warhorses like 'Falling In Love Again' (Marlene Dietrich's signature tune), Noël Coward's title track and a 'Mack The Knife' that was as downbeat as Bobby Darin's 1959 chart-topper wasn't.

The mid-1990s saw the publication too of Faithfull's eponymous autobiography, an intriguing companion tome for Stones enthusiasts to Marsha Hunt's similarly candid *Real Life*. However, Chrissie Shrimpton's attempt to tell her side of the story was thwarted by Jagger's injunction preventing her from quoting from his now dog-eared letters to her.

It seemed to be open season on Mick. Keith, referring to him privately as 'Brenda' – after Brenda Jagger's English book shop in Paris – surmised that 'he doesn't have many close male friends, apart from me, and he keeps me at a distance. There is something of a siege mentality, so that, whenever anyone comes up to Mick, he's thinking, "What do they want out of me?"'[2] Self-protecting psychological tactics were, if you like, in keeping with a characteristic of Aries, his astrological sign, and few could ever gauge whether he'd be hail-fellow-well-met or stonewalling towards them. 'I'd be with him from ten in the morning until ten at night,' affirmed David Sanderson, a latter-day Stones employee, 'but the next day, he'd behave almost as if we'd never met before – like, "Who are you, and who are you calling 'Mick'?"'

It wasn't advisable to put on such airs with Jeff Beck, who Mick transparently hoped would join him on the road as well as on disc, as a Jagger tour of Japan was on the cards for the beginning of 1988, with Australasia and a side-trip to Indonesia scheduled for the autumn, prior, presumably, to cracking the harder nut of North America. Jeff's participation seemed likely, as he'd been game enough to let himself be seen in the video for 'Throwaway', the second single from *Primitive Cool*, the album hot on the heels of *She's The Boss*.

Primitive Cool had smouldered into form under the aegis of the co-writer of three of the ten tracks, Dave Stewart, better known as half of The Eurythmics, a post-punk combo whose musical policy and subsequent chart entries had been founded on a truce between synthesiser trickery and minor-key human emotion. New advances in studio technology informed *Primitive Cool*, too, as did the input of minds younger than Stewart's, among them personnel from black New York ensemble Living Colour. Impressed by their stint in a city club, Jagger had overseen the tape that had procured Living Colour a recording deal. Paying close attention to what made the now-teenage Karis and Jade groove, he had also assisted on the album *Strange Things* from Tackhead, a local hip-hop collective. His recreational listening lay in the same direction, and he reiterated that he'd fallen out of love with 'traditional rock music. I've done it to death.'[3]

Jagger was just as scornful about aspects of 'new tradition', a new development in country and western. Though it was finding favour with young consumers by rescuing C&W from its rhinestoned tackiness, Mick, while confessing that he didn't mind Dwight Yoakam and Ofra Haza, found Randy Travis 'deadly dull, this year's Jim Reeves, but all the girls like Randy'.[4]

As much as demonstrative awareness of modern pop, a major ingredient in the *Primitive Cool* cauldron was his lyrical soul-baring – that he'd found true love after a lifelong search in 'Throwaway'; a dig at Keith in 'Shoot Off Your Mouth', while fielding questions from the children about his past in the title song – inviting fair-to-middling critiques, typified by *Q*'s 'an improvement...respectable but not *earthed*'.[5] For once, these views were reflected in chart positions, with the inaugural single – bolt-upright 'Let's Work' – entering at Number 35 in Britain and rising no further, despite Mick taking the trouble to plug it with a *Top Of The Pops* slot that was more like an Eileen Fowler keep-fit class.

A recent hit, however modest, still kept him in the public eye, and two shows at Tokyo's 55,000-capacity Kerakuen Dome – the biggest venue on the Japanese itinerary – sold out on the day they were announced. For the second of these, Tina Turner's presence was an unexpected pleasure for the fans[6] as she jogged on to join in 'Brown Sugar' and 'It's Only Rock 'n' Roll'.

For some, this guest appearance made up for the non-appearance of Jeff Beck, then recovering from a domestic accident that had almost cost him the thumb on his left hand. This mishap, nevertheless, wasn't why he'd cried off; the warning signs had been the inventive but petulant Jeff's disgruntlement at the *Primitive Cool* selections being presented to him and the other musicians as more of a *fait accompli* than had been the case on *She's The Boss*. 'I wanted to be in an experimental Rolling Stones with Jagger singing,' he gloomed, 'and I was sure that was what he wanted, but as time drifted by, I realised he was determined to put the songs on tape the way he wanted them. He wanted a very stylised album. I was just slotted in as a guest, a studio-type guy.'[7]

Beck was bemused too by the large amount of old material in the proposed set list for the tour: 'It turned out there were 15 Rolling Stones songs, and I didn't want to go to Australia and Japan to play a load of Keith Richards licks.'[7] Neither did the ace guitarist wish to skulk beyond the main spotlight as one of a backing band in which 'we were all planetary kinds of people'[7] – which, though named The Brothers Of Sodom, included 'two chicks prancing around doing "Tumbling Dice"', raged Keith Richards. 'It was very sad that a high percentage of his show was Stones songs. If you're going to do stuff on your own, do stuff off the two albums you did.'[8] Perhaps this was erring on the side of caution by a Jagger who, moments before his Japanese concert debut, had come nearly as close to vomiting with nerves as he had before that hesitant 'Around And Around' with Blues Incorporated back in nineteen-sixty-forget-about-it.

Of the same vintage was 'the four-headed monster' – so Mick had quipped when coaxing representatives of The Beatles George and Ringo, plus John's widow and elder son – saying a few words at 1988's annual Rock 'n' Roll Hall Of Fame gala in the banqueting room of New York's Waldorf-Astoria Hotel. Then Jagger made his way back onto the stage for the 'surprise' all-star blow at the end, bunching around a single microphone with Harrison and Bob Dylan for a raucous 'I Saw Her Standing There'. The strains of 'Like A Rolling Stone', led by Dylan and Jagger, and 'Satisfaction', with Jagger and Jeff Beck to the fore also dominated the joyous proceedings.

Eighteen months earlier, Mick had been on camera too at a Prince's Trust Concert at Wembley Pool, delivering 'Dancing In The Street' with Bowie. Yet he never quite became one of the usual shower – Eric Clapton, Elton John, Annie Lennox, Phil Collins *et al* – expected to show their faces on such occasions as a contrast to the processed frenzy of Curiosity Killed The Cat, Bros, Wet Wet Wet and other Me Generation chart-riders.

Nevertheless, Jagger laid out a dry-cleaned suit, shampooed his hair and polished his shoes on 18 January 1989 when it was The Rolling Stones' turn to be inducted into Rock 'n' Roll Hall Of Fame. With him on the podium stood Keith, Ron Wood and Mick Taylor, and, on their behalf, he made the acceptance speech, cracking, 'It's slightly ironic that tonight you see us on our best behaviour, but we've been awarded for 25 years of bad behaviour.' He also paid tribute to Brian Jones and the more recently deceased Ian Stewart.

The news prompted Dick Taylor to meditate further about what might have been. From his home on the Isle of Wight, he was commuting to his Pretty Things duties and other professional engagements, like him and Phil May pitching in on 1990's *United*, the second album by the British Invasion All-Stars, an amalgam of founder members of The Yardbirds, The Downliners Sect, The Creation and The Nashville Teens. 'Dick turned out one great effortless riff after another,' marvelled the Sect's Don Craine, 'and Phil, arriving like a 1950s screen idol, put most songs down in one take. Pretty, they weren't; brilliant, they were and are.'

Another All-Star, Yardbird Jim McCarty, would recount that a few months later, 'It was the idea of George Paulus, a US music historian, for Dick, Phil and I to record some R&B in a Chicago studio with US musicians – like Richard Hite, bass player from Canned Heat – and breathe the same air as Howlin' Wolf, Muddy Waters and all the Chess legends. We taped a lot of Bo Diddley, Chuck Berry – all the usual stuff – and a great version of Aretha

Franklin's 'Chain Of Fools'. While we were there, we also managed a few club gigs, every one of them packed out, despite the freezing cold and constant blizzards.'

Back home, as well as R&B oldies on the juke-box, on the disco turntable and in bar-band repertoire, some of their original perpetrators would still be labouring to set up equipment at opening time – as was true of 50-something John Mayall at London's Town and Country Club, where, though his name had been misspelled on the ticket, he was as ecstatic as his cramped devotees that he was so rabidly remembered.

That demand for the old music – and the old musicians – was still potent was a V-sign at everything Keith Richards detested about mainstream pop these days – including what he called 'Mick's high-tech records'.[9] It also gave Jagger pause for thought. In Japan and Australasia, all the majority of customers wanted to hear were the sounds of yesteryear, as the poorer sales for *Primitive Cool* – and, *Talk Is Cheap*, a solo LP Keith had put out in 1988 – against *Rewind* and its by-products testified. If the next Mick Jagger album – if there was to be one – gave the profit graph another downward turn, what then?

How could Mick possibly have visualised too the loneliness and disappointment that his breaking free had brought him? As for Keith, he had channelled some of his disenchantment with the Stones' disintegration into reactivating the waning careers of certain of his boyhood idols, realizing his wildest dream via his organisation of an all-star backing group for a televised concert starring Chuck Berry – who, Keith had to admit grudgingly, 'gave me more headaches than Mick Jagger'.[8]

Both Mick and Keith had, therefore, experienced different revelations that arrived at the same conclusion: that there was to be no more circling around the issue with solo ventures. They anchored themselves to the notion that they were going to be Rolling Stones once more, and would have to put up with constantly being told that their best work was behind them. Significantly, The

Counterfeit Stones – a 'tribute band' then in formation – rehearsed nothing beyond the mid-1970s.

It was easier to let go, stop trying to prove themselves, get out of step with the strident march of computer-proficient hip-hop, techno, acid house *et al*, and go back to making music that felt like it was hanging on a thread. It was pointless, reckoned Keith, for Mick to 'keep looking back over his shoulder at Michael Jackson, Prince and George Michael. I've told him it's ludicrous to try to pretend you're 20 when you're 45.'[9] Like a cat that has tried in vain to catch a mouse before walking away as if he'd never had any such an idea, Jagger seemed to be refuting his forays into the latest sounds: 'It's not that I don't like that music. I just don't think it has any relevance within the Stones. Maybe I'm old-fashioned, but I don't think the writing – certainly the lyric writing – is particularly interesting.'[4] He had a point. Some exponents were given to either repeating one line *ad nauseam* or just 'emoting' wordlessly whenever rhymes and scansion seemed too much like hard work.

Outstanding solo commitments were yet to be fulfilled when the Stones convened at London's Savoy Hotel on 18 May 1988 to see if a regrouping was actually tenable. There were moments when the meeting was more like corporation presidents discussing a merger than five old friends wanting to play together again. Yet, perversely, with the pressure of the next album no longer looming, Jagger and Richards had found themselves working out chord changes and words for several new songs that sounded more Stones than *Primitive Cool* or *Talk Is Cheap*.

These and others that came later were to fill *Steel Wheels*, the recording of which was notable for its accomplishing more in one evening than in the weeks of retakes and scrapped tracks that had had to be endured for albums in the bad old days. 'In the past, we've spent too long looking at the ceiling, getting really frustrated, waiting for the great inspiration,' explained Mick. 'It makes for very long, drawn-out sessions with not particularly good results. This inevitably leads to friction within the band.'[4]

The unadorned production criteria and sparser ensemble work coincided with a world-wide resurgence of garage bands, who recorded in defiantly anachronistic mono, if possible, and performed with a thrillingly retrogressive and riff-based verve that married rockabilly and punk thrash to veneration for rock's elder statesmen. Indeed, a packed-out garage-band extravaganza in north London was to culminate with the UK stage debut of ? And The Mysterions, excavated from their Michigan obscurity to walk a taut, if limited, artistic tightrope.

Likewise, The Pretty Things – fresh from a well-received US tour with The Loons, San Diego's boss garage band – were assisted by the UK's Inmates on *A Whiter Shade Of Dirty Water*, a rewinding of pop history whereby they powered through the best-known songs by ? And The Mysterions, The Strangeloves, The Chocolate Watch Band and other US Anglophiles that they – and the Stones – had inspired during the British Invasion. With the masters at work, it was almost a matter of course that '96 Tears', 'I Want Candy', 'Let's Talk About Girls' and all the rest of them would be played with more guts than the callow apprentices managed during recorded sound's medieval era, with Dick and Phil still sounding as abandoned as they did in 1964. Recommended unconditionally to anyone who prefers The Downliners Sect to Living Colour, the new wave of garage-band music bore roughly the same parallel to such acts as the strict oil-on-canvas tenets of Stuckism (or remodernism) would to Brit Art, with its Turner Prize-nominated dead sheep and unmade bed.

You weren't sure either how you were meant to take the emerging tribute bands that had cloned the Stones. Complete with a lead vocalist with the *nom de théâtre* 'Nick Dagger', The Counterfeit Stones – 'probably the second greatest rock 'n' roll band of all time', boasted their publicity spiel – were the oldest and most popular. Other copycats included The Rolling Clones, recipients of a stern letter from a firm representing the genuine article, demanding that they drop their name and stop using the tongue-and-lips logo.

For all Mick's chicken neck and Keith's headband almost disguising a 'good' forehead, the real Stones in the 1990s remained a source of fascination for the young – and not-so-young – envious of their unquiet journey towards pensionable age. Hence, if not as content to exalt and imitate them as the tribute bands, The Membranes gladly retrod 'Angie'; Mike Sweeney And His Thunderbyrds' '19th Nervous Breakdown', and The Primeval Unknown 'Jumpin' Jack Flash' when helping to fill needle-time on *Stoned Again*, a compilation of chosen reworkings from the Stones' portfolio.

Stoned Again crept into the Top Ten of the *NME*'s independent album chart just as the group that had activated it embarked on a world tour that would prove the most lucrative in pop history. Breaking all previous records, the box office at the Sullivan Stadium in Boston cleared 150,000 tickets in under seven hours.

18 My Bitter Seed

'Spending a lot of time on the road is different from most people's experience, but my parents protected me from whatever wild antics were going on. My father has got a great work ethic, and he's always been an example.'

– Jade Jagger[1]

They warmed up for the *Steel Wheels* tour in front of a lucky few hundred in New Haven's Toad's Night Club; 55 minutes on its small stage was roughly like a Channel swimmer crossing Dover harbour a few times. On the road, Mick would have to pace himself over three hours before a vast backdrop of his own devising ('quite industrial, quite moody'[2]), taking breathers when his movements were restricted by stints on rhythm guitar and – to a greater degree – during Keith's solitary lead vocal outing.

Girls gasped rather than screamed when Mick took his shirt off now, but they still expected him to sweat away pounds with his cavortings, goading himself, the group and, vicariously, his onlookers to near collapse. Never sacrificing impassioned content for technical virtuosity, he drew from an arsenal of facial expressions, flickering hand ballets and more exertive antics – plus enhancements such as the inflatable Rottweiler that swallowed him during 'Street Fighting Man' – as he bombarded the audience with the characters and scenarios of the songs. 'Offstage, the problem is keeping your feet on the ground,' he mused. 'It's very, very difficult. You do get very prima-donna-ish and very wrapped up in your own inflated ego.'[2]

No opera diva was more pampered. Daily voice-coaching sessions were yet to come, but his body was massaged by Dorothy 'Dr Dot' Stein – as illustrious in her field as he was in his – and his make-up was applied by the similarly highly waged Pierre Laroche, who also serviced David Bowie, Sophia Loren, Joan Collins, Charlotte Rampling, Anjelica Houston – you name 'em. 'If someone has droopy eyes,' explained Laroche, 'I will work at making them even droopier. If someone has a big nose, I will emphasise that nose.'[3] It is possible to guess which of Jagger's features received such attention.

Max Bygraves and Ted Rogers lived on in US comedienne Joan Rivers, who delivered a televised monologue centred on Mick and his 'child-bearing lips' in the midst of a *Steel Wheels* expedition that touched its home base in summer 1990. One of three Wembley Stadium concerts coincided with a World Cup soccer match involving England, splitting the concentration of both those with transistor radios glued to their ears and those onstage, especially when a sudden burst of cheering (when England scored) punctuated a hush between numbers.

Yet the local-boys-made-good's time on the boards flew by as quickly as the reading of the most page-turning thriller, and they pulled a far bigger audience than Frank Sinatra crooning to 7,000 on plastic seats at the London Arena that same night. Moreover, the Stones were to finish the year voted the Greatest Rockers Of All Time in a poll taken by US periodical *Entertainment Weekly*, with Bob Dylan and The Beatles in second and third place.

With a new album, *Voodoo Lounge*, demonstrating that there was life in the old dogs yet, both artistically and commercially, the momentum hadn't slackened when the Stones toured again, in 1994. Moreover, as *USA Today* noted, Mick's voice was 'deeper and throatier now, but still a yowling menace, unmellowed by age'.[4]

It was also the first jaunt without Bill Wyman. A night off during a Pretty Things trek round The Netherlands found Bill's predecessor renewing acquaintance with his old comrades in the VIP enclosure of a Stones recital on a festival site near Brussels.

The millennia since 1962 were brushed aside like so much chaff during Dick Taylor's conversation, when the fury was subsiding, with his Dartford Grammar classmate, who was, so Dick observed, 'still pretty much the same person he always was'.

Neither had Mick gone so far beyond that he couldn't dare a hiking holiday in Wales with his father and son, or lend a hand when brother Chris took another stab at pop fame – after a vinyl silence of nigh on 20 years – with 1994's *Atcha*, an album with Mick on 'Stand Up For The Fool' (about which he commented, 'Blimey, that's fast!').[5] While the elder brother declined to pitch in during the valedictory jam session of ancient R&B, he didn't conduct himself like visiting royalty when, dressed down, he and Chris showed their faces in the back room of Putney's Half-Moon pub, its ceiling yellow with decades of rising cigarette smoke, for a benefit gig for the bereaved family of one of Keith's minders. He even clapped politely when Hugh Cornwell – once of the detested Stranglers – approximated one of their hits.

Yet, no matter how much Jagger soft-pedalled his measureless celebrity, England's cricket XI were delighted to have their picture taken with him – and national newspapers to publish it – and the Stones were judged by Richard Branson to be 'Mick Jagger plus three others'[6] when, after periodic attempts since 1975, he signed them to his Virgin label in 1991. It would be Atlantic, however, that would press Jagger's *Wandering Spirit*, a solo album of more downbeat kidney than its predecessors. While it included a revival of James Brown's 'Think', the traditional *Lied* 'Handsome Molly' was its finale, symptomatic of an abiding interest in folk music that would also rear up when the Stones contributed to 1995's *Long Black Veil* by The Chieftains, the most renowned ambassadors of Celtic music, although accused by pedants of emasculating their art via other artistic alliances with Frank Zappa, Roger Daltrey and Van Morrison.

If *Wandering Spirit*'s singles – self-penned 'Sweet Thing', 'Don't Tear Me Up' and 'Out Of Focus' – spread themselves thinly enough to be worthwhile marketing exercises without actually troubling the charts, the album made the most commercial headway of all Jagger's solo ventures – in Europe, anyway – gaining a gold disc in Germany, the world's third most vital sales territory, and slicing to Number Five in Britain.

Things were looking up on celluloid, too. Mick had been a selling point for 1992's science-fiction fantasy *Freejack* as a sort of loveable villain, his first role since *Fitzcarraldo*. In no mood to worry about whether or not he remained the draw he'd been in the *Performance/Ned Kelly* era, he was quite happy about a supporting role to Sir Anthony Hopkins, then on the rebound from *The Silence Of The Lambs*. However, the general verdict was that Jagger had coped well enough with a comparatively undemanding part in a so-so movie.

Hitherto untapped talents in the realm of moving pictures were to surface when he set up his own production company, Jagged Films, in 1996. He seemed particularly keen on bio-pics, having acquired the rights three years earlier to a treatment of rural blues legend Robert Johnson's eventful 24 years on this planet. Then there was a trip to Colombia in connection with the life and death of Che Guevara, along with earnest discussion about Dylan Thomas. Purportedly, Jagger himself came up with a screenplay for a film based on his own experiences in a 1960s pop group. In 2001, however, Jagged Productions actually completed a film: a Tom Stoppard adaptation of Robert Harris's best-selling World War II adventure, *Enigma*. As with Alfred Hitchcock, the sharp-eyed would spot Mick in minor cameos in *Enigma*, *The Man From Elysian Fields* and further flicks, but, to date, he hasn't taken another role as big as even *Freejack*, let alone *Performance*.

Mick's quasi-swashbuckling antics in *Freejack* belied the onset of middle age. In a couple of years, he'd qualify to be a new face, if he desired, at the Over Fifties sessions in Richmond's Municipal Swimming Pool. From the town Mick used to know rose the eminence overlooking the Thames where the future George IV had courted Mrs Fitzherbert, the 'sweet lass of Richmond Hill'. The wealthy had had residences erected there since the 16th century. Downe House, one such mansion, had just been purchased by the Jaggers.

While his brother contemplated a dotage rich in material comforts, Chris Jagger – no spring-chicken, either – was scratching a living from his pen, writing for *The Oldie*, amongst other publications. Furthermore, Jade and her boyfriend were to make Mick and Bianca grandparents with the coming of Assisi in, well, Assisi, Italy, in 1992. Adding to genealogical complexities, the baby's aunt – Georgia May Ayeesha, born to Jerry on 12 January 1992 – was still in nappies herself when Jade presented Mick with a second granddaughter, Amba, three years later, and Jerry bore a second son, Gabriel Luke Beauregard, in London on 9 December 1997.

Mick wasn't present during his wife's latest confinement in a London hospital, as he was away on tour, getting up to she knew not what, as he pondered again the old puzzle of how other men managed to direct both love and desire to the same woman all their wedded lives. A lady of perennially good nature – and once 'the other woman' herself – Jerry was abstractedly tolerant of – or indifferent to – printed murmurings about Mick's faraway escapades as he rediscovered his taste for illicit sex. So far, none had impinged upon the marriage, but awkward questions were asked in 1999 when Brazilian model Luciana Morad named Mick – correctly – as the father of her new-born boy, Lucas, and demanded financial settlement for his upbringing.

The resulting tabloid commotion was one of amusement rather than the stirring up of lynch-mob fever that had underlined Gary Glitter's fall when he was jailed for accumulating images of child pornography culled from the Internet. 'GIVE US A KISS, YOU OLD ROGUE!' sniggered one such rag when Hall was snapped embracing her sinful man at some society function or other. There were also stray paragraphs about a second honeymoon; about a penitence expressed, apparently, through pleading letters posted during another Stones journey round the globe; and about Mick watching with observed good humour on the opening night of *The Graduate*, a West End adaptation of the 1967 sex comedy – this time starring Jerry as the seductive 'Mrs Robinson' – which, during one act, required her to stand nude in dim light, just as Marsha Hunt had done in *Hair*.

Mick was more open about any misgivings when, through the agency of their mother, Elizabeth – and then James, after a small beginning in a fashion show at school – made debuts on the catwalk. It was a springboard to an income of up to half a million pounds a year for Elizabeth, while her brother ended up being cited in 2003 as one of the kingdom's most eligible bachelors in *Tatler*'s end-of-year roundup.

As is a teenager's wont, James also attracted complaints from neighbours – and the attention of the media – for spinning loud music on his stereo one afternoon when his parents were out, while Georgia's exposed midriff in restaurants warranted her mother's disapproval. Not yet 20, Elizabeth caused greater concern about the unsuitability of one of her young men – or not so young, as it happened. However, after 44-year-old actor Michael Wincott, she walked out with 28-year-old Sean Lennon, who, beamed Jerry, 'looks so like John now, and writes beautiful poetry'.[7] A chip off the old block, Sean held his own when fingering piano during musical *soirées*, known as 'Jerry's Jam Sessions', at Downe House with the likes of Pete Townshend, Bob Geldof – and Bill Wyman, still *persona grata* with Mick. It was Bill's idea for Jerry to 'talk-sing' two *risqué* numbers from the 1920s, 'I'll Let You Play With My Little Yo-Yo' and ''Cos It Feels So Good', as a novelty single out in time for 2004's December sell-in.

Royalties earned by Jerry from this diversion were a mere bagatelle compared to those from her numerous stage appearances since *Bus Stop*, most impressively as 'Calamity Jane' in Dorothy Squires' one-woman play *My Darling Janey*, based on letters written by the gun-slinging heroine. Just as Mae West had been synonymous with 'Diamond Lil' in the 1927 Broadway presentation of the same name, so Jerry Hall *was* Calamity Jane – or at least aspects of her were. 'Like every Texan girl,' she grinned, 'I spent a lot of time shooting tin cans.'[8]

In the months leading up to her divorce, Jerry had also spent a lot of time 'constantly slaying dragons. He kept me in a state of confusion, with all the turmoil and drama.'[9] Yet, while there'd been some legal nastiness about the legality of their wedding in Bali, the two behaved amicably enough, even lovingly, when they were together. To separate completely was unthinkable, and both continued to live at Downe House where, if Jerry preferred Mick not to bed his latest girlfriend there, Lucas came to be regarded as one of an extended family as much as the children by Marsha and Bianca.

His and Hunt's daughter, Karis was as North American as she was English. Barely able to contain his pride, Mick had attended her graduation at Yale in 1992, and helped in any way he could her pursuit of a chosen career in film. After a period in front of the camera – notably in *One Night Stand*, brainchild of Mike Figgis – Karis became a director, overseeing her own mother in a turn-of-the-millennium movie.

Mick had instilled into all his brood what ought to be admired about achievement by effort. Taking this to heart, Jade – now in her 30s – was thriving as creative director for Garrard's, jewellers by royal appointment, with branches in Mayfair and Manhattan. Of all Jagger offspring, she thrust her head highest above the parapet, socially too. In September 2003, one of the highlights of London Fashion Week was Jade Jagger's party, where the entertainment was at its most eye-stretching with a peekaboo burlesque routine performed by the lady love of US shock-rocker Marilyn Manson.

Since the infancy of her children, Jade's paramours had included a nephew of Camilla Parker-Bowles – the Prince of Wales's 'significant other' – but she'd settled with British musician Dan Williams on a self-sustaining farm to the north of the island of Ibiza, whilst renting a converted warehouse in London, where she made an imperious Grand Entrance into the city's Wellington Club, announcing to the doorman that she was 'Jade, first-born [sic] child of Mick Jagger, the Son of God'.[10]

Dad was not, however, the messiah he used to be, what with the Stones' most recent British spectaculars being scorned by *The Times* as being 'a cross between Billy Smart's Circus and a *Saga* convention'.[11] Though his 30-minute performance in Los Angeles's El Rey Theater to launch a fourth solo album was an industry event, *Goddess In The Doorway* sold in thousands rather than tens of thousands until the broadcast of a television documentary, *Being Mick*, an interlacing of studio and domestic scenes from a stay in Mustique with family members such as father Joe, now widowed since 87-year-old Eva's death in 2000. Her sons had sung the spiritual 'Will The Circle Be Unbroken' at the funeral service at St Andrew's Church, not far from Downe House.

One of the last major gatherings of the clan had been in a Thanet hotel for Joe and Eva's golden wedding anniversary in 1990. Since then, Mick had been prone to plunging into occasional orgies of reminiscence about his old home town. Indeed, he became something of a patrician, presenting Maypole Primary School with a computer and endorsing the naming of the Mick Jagger Performing Arts Centre on the site of the grammar school. He'd been standing by with his parents as the Duke of Kent snipped the ribbon at its opening on Thursday 30 March 2000, after which a local outfit named Cherry Sunburst cranked out 'Brown Sugar' on the polished pinewood stage.

The tentacles of Mick's altruism were thrust beyond Dartford when he donated the synthesiser upon which he and Keith had composed *Steel Wheels* selections to Instruments Amnesty, a children's music charity. Long before that, it had been reported that Jagger had put his hand in his pocket to sponsor Britain's gymnastic team for the Los Angeles Olympic Games, partly to please his father and partly as a 'backing Britain' gesture.

What was his game? If he had one, it was to attain its end in June 2002, when Prime Minister Tony Blair advised Princess Margaret's sister to grant the showbusiness icon a knighthood. A self-styled 'guy', Blair had been lead singer in an amateur rock group called Ugly Rumours when he'd been every inch the long-haired hippy student with prog-rock albums on instant replay on his hostel-room stereo.

Jagger's investiture was, Blair said, for 'services to music' – because, as well as being the most public face of The Rolling Stones, in 1991, he and London-based promoter Harvey Goldsmith had persuaded the arts ministry – with the approbation of Equity – to inaugurate an annual National Music Day, to be filled with festivals, concerts and eisteddfods across the land. Mick was much in evidence in celebratory newspaper articles, though he declined to be photographed with Screaming Lord Sutch – the longest-serving party leader in British politics – at one open-air event. Impending knighthood bred fine sensibilities.

To many, nevertheless, the notion of 'Sir Mick Jagger' was as absurd as that of Prime Minister Sutch. More palatable was his personal letter of support to Boris Yeltsin after the failed counter-rebellion to Glasnost. This helped clear the way for Jagger's election in 1994 as honorary president of the LSE Students' Union. Among the runners-up was the beatified Mother Teresa of Calcutta.

A dash of religion would further embellish Mick's elevation to national treasure. A red string tied around his wrist indicated an adherence to a form of *kabbalah*, a pantheistic doctrine that had allured as many famous converts as the Maharishi had in 1967. Most of them – Barbra Streisand, Elizabeth Taylor, Anjelica Houston[12] and Britney Spears, to name but four – were female, but Mick's friend, photographer David Bailey proclaimed himself a follower, even if footballer David Beckham dismissed his own string bracelet as a simple fashion statement.

Kabbalah's principal text is the Zohar, essentially a chronicle of visions received by Jewish mystics thousands of years ago. It delved too into numerology, astrology, meditation and pre-Christian methods of anger management. Yet cult leader Rabbi Philip Berg – a former insurance salesman – taught that it was feasible to understand the ancient text by merely running your fingers over it.

Mick – and Jerry – went so far as to organise a fundraising dinner in Berg's honour at South Kensington's Harrington Club, but there have since been no public statements from either about indoctrination, possibly because Berg – like the Maharishi – required the titheing of a percentage of each initiate's income.

Such displays of unity with her ex-husband extended to Jerry's continued presence at Stones extravaganzas, where 'he still mesmerises me. I'm like, wow! Just like the rest of the fans.'⁹ Yet she was otherwise engaged when Mick, soberly attired, was driven at last to Buckingham Palace on 12 December 2003 to kneel before Prince Charles and have his shoulders tapped with a ceremonial sword. Outside the great double doors to the chandeliered royal drawing room, he grinned at Gerry of the Pacemakers and Procol Harum's Gary Brooker, there to receive lesser honours.

Facing the press in the courtyard afterwards, press cameras caught the flash of a diamond-studded front molar as he smiled again while opining, 'I don't think the Establishment we knew exists any more.'¹³

A few hours later, the noise of the subsequent celebration lacerated the night air outside the Temple, a club founded by the first Viscount Astor in the 19th century. Less than a mile away, a listed building that had once been Marlborough Street Magistrates' Court had opened as the five-star Courthouse Hotel in July 2004. The cell in which Mick Jagger had been taken to await one of his drugs trials now caters for up to eight diners, who use what had been its toilet as a champagne bucket.

Epilogue
Odds And Ends

'Even in these multi-millionaire times, when the rebel consorts with the aristocracy and meets them on his own terms, Jagger is still one of the most important and enduring of the rock gods – and that's not an easy thing for a white lad from Dartford.'

– Frank Allen of The Searchers[1]

This is probably a silly hypothetical exercise, but let's cross to a parallel dimension for a moment and read a feature on the entertainments page of the 23 October 2005 edition of the *Kentish Times*:

WHO SAID THEY'D NEVER LAST?

As The Pretty Things cruise by limousine to Wembley during the UK leg of their record-breaking world tour, their old rivals, The Rolling Stones, take the stage to a small but appreciative crowd at Eltham's Jolly Fenman. The group had no qualms about mining seams other than rhythm and blues. Motown, classic rock, jazz, and mainstream pop mingled with set works like 'I Ain't Got You' and a 'Roll Over Beethoven' that led one member of a near-capacity audience to remove his shirt and cavort crazily, probably belying a daytime sobriety as a stock-controller or school janitor.

With only Mick Jagger and Keith Richards left from

the original lineup, this was the group's first booking after a long lay-off – one of many during 30 years of bad luck, administrative chicanery, excessive record-company thrift and Jagger being typecast as a poor man's Phil May.

There'd been a place in the pub-rock sun for the latter-day Stones back in the mid-1970s, and they'd picked up a neo-punk audience who bought reissues of the old LPs. 1967's psychedelic 'Citadel' even made the 'alternative' chart in *Sounds*, and a German label commissioned a new Stones album, *It Should Have Been Us*.

Of course, it couldn't last, and a schedule that had once signified a week's work became a month's. Apart from compilations built around their handful of beat-boom Top 50 entries, the only new Stones commodity during the next decade was 1986's *Live At The Station Tavern* – though, more recently, Mick shook his trademark maracas on an EP by Thee Headcoats, one of the mainstays of the Medway towns indie scene. Nevertheless, there's every reason to suppose that, sooner rather than later, they'll be providing another of these 'greatest nights anyone could ever remember' at a venue near you. Don't miss it!

Unreal life wasn't like that for Mick Jagger and The Rolling Stones. Instead, they all but overtook The Beatles as the showbusiness sensation of the 1960s. Crucially, most of the Stones' raw material was strong enough to withstand accusations of borrowing conveniently trendy gimmicks from the Fab Four; 'Paint It Black' worked just as well as a 1967 A-side by Chris Farlowe, produced by Jagger, who traded Brian Jones's sitar for an eastern European setting, complete with gypsy violins and a syncopated *bolero* passage. Moreover, if reduced to the acid test of just voice and piano or guitar, 'Have You Seen Your Mother' isn't much of a song in retrospect – and neither is 'The Ballad Of John And Yoko' – but 'Jumpin' Jack Flash' surfaces more frequently than 'Yesterday', for all its syndications, as a pop evergreen on nostalgia radio, and as frequently in 'Sounds Of The '60s' nights as 'Yesterday' does in 'quality' cabaret.

And in the end, by concentrating on the possible, the Stones won the game, in the sense that they far outlasted The Beatles. Furthermore, although Seneca reminds us that 'life is all the more delightful when it is on the downward slope', they continue to break box-office records and sustain chart-making interest – just – with their latest output, while Ringo Starr follows the nostalgia trail and Paul McCartney overpaints his artistic canvas.

Inevitably, advancing age has taken its toll. Jagger had a health scare in 1991 – a lump on his pelvis that was later revealed to be a benign cyst – and 13 years later 63-year-old Charlie Watts was diagnosed with throat cancer. Less seriously, the crux of a well-received play entitled *Finding Mick Jagger* in 2004's Edinburgh Festival was a 50-something's obsessive determination to make contact with his idol in order to convince him that he must retire.

'I can't see us stopping,' parried Mick. 'Maybe we won't tour as we did – 16 months non-stop – but more regularly. I don't like to stay away from the stage too long, but I don't see us just as a live act. I think we have to do a record soon. Being a live band gives you instant gratification. Records don't.'[2]

For all his artistic *faux pas* and rose-tinted memories of 'Satisfaction', and even 'Start Me Up', much of Jagger's output since – both with the Stones and as a solo artist – has been far less objectionable than the increasingly bland offerings of some of his more commercially viable contemporaries.

Yet, while 'Old Habits Die Hard' – the single from the score he co-wrote to *Alfie*, an Americanised remake of the Swinging '60s film comedy – was poised to penetrate autumn 2004's domestic Top 20, all the old Stones singles are scheduled to be issued on CD in boxed sets of ten. Massive sales are anticipated, bolstering not so much an argument but plain fact that, whatever their makers have got up to since the decade of their maximum impact, most of it has been barely relevant. To certain of their still countless devotees, it was the Stones' misfortune not to have either vanished altogether from public life after 'Jumpin' Jack Flash' or to have joined Brian Jones in the depths of his swimming pool.

Notes

In addition to my own correspondence and notes, I have used the following sources, which I would like to credit:

Prologue: Big Boss Man

1 *Melody Maker*, 23 April 1966
2 *Real Life* by M Hunt (Chatto & Windus, 1986)
3 *Stone Alone* by B Wyman and R Coleman (Viking, 1990)
4 *The Stones* by P Norman (Sidgwick & Jackson, 2001)
5 *Up And Down With The Rolling Stones* by T Sanchez and J Blake (Blake Paperbacks, 1991)
6 *Arise, Sir Mick: The True Story Of Britain's Naughtiest Knight* by L Jackson (Trafalgar Square, 2004)
7 *Our Own Story* by P Goodman (Beat Publications, 1964)

1 Go On To School

1 *Woman's World*, 19 April 1982
2 *Who's Who In Popular Music In Britain*, ed S Tracy (World's Work, 1984)
3 *The Times*, 18 July 2003
4 And was still being called Mike in a *New Musical Express* article published on 28 February 1964
5 Sleeve notes for *The Chuck Berry London Sessions* (Chess, 1972)
6 *Sunday Times*, 1990 (precise date obscured)
7 *New Musical Express*, 2 September 1989
8 *Evening Post*, 28 December 1989

2 Boogie In The Dark

1 *Jeff Beck: Crazy Fingers* by A Carson (Carson, 1998)

2 Scottish author and musician Jim Wilkie would later argue that it owed much to the Gaels who colonised the southern states during the late 18th century. See his *Blue Suede Brogans* (Mainstream, 1991)

3 *Best Of Guitar Player*, Rolling Stones special, December 1993

4 *The Land Where The Blues Began* by A Lomax (Minerva, 1999)

5 See chapter headings

6 *A Guide To Popular Music* by P Gammond and P Clayton (Phoenix, 1960)

7 Quoted in an interview with Chris Jagger (*New Musical Express*, 25 June 1965)

8 *New Musical Express*, 1 November 1957

9 *The Times*, 18 July 2003

10 'Eggheads' by Bryan Blackburn and Peter Reeves (Philips, PB 1171, 1961)

11 *Howling At The Moon* by W Yetnikoff and D Ritz (Abacus, 2004)

3 Outskirts Of Town

1 *Rolling Stones In Their Own Words*, ed D Dalton and M Farren (Omnibus, 1985)

2 The group included Patrick Kerr, future presenter on ITV's *Ready Steady Go* pop series.

3 *London Live* by T Bacon (Balafon, 1999)

4 With an awesome contempt for historical and cultural context, one of Dick Taylor's flatmates taped over it in 1965

5 Harpo's 'Shake Your Hips' was in Jagger's G Club repertoire. It was to be dusted off for The Rolling Stones' 1972 double album, *Exile On Main Street*

6 *Days In The Life*, ed J Green (Heinemann, 1988)

7 *Alexis Korner* by H Shapiro (Bloomsbury, 1996)

8 *Midland Beat*, No 10, July 1963

9 The expression 'rollin' stone' was also contained in a line from a field recording made before Waters migrated to Chicago. Moreover, 'Rollin' Stone' was a minor US hit in 1958 for The Marigolds (formerly The Prisonaires)

10 *Jazz News*, 21 November 1962)

4 Bright Lights, Big City

1 *Rock Explosion* by H Bronson (Blandford, 1986)

2 Through whose ranks would pass Rod Stewart

3 *The British Invasion* by B Harry (Chrome Dreams, 2004)

4 *Q*, May 1995

5 The Moon Is Rising

1 From 'Wake Up In The Morning', a 30-second jingle for an ITV commercial commissioned early in 1964 by Kellogg's. Its composition was attributed to

Brian Jones and a lyricist from an advertising agency

2   *Jazz News*, 21 November 1962

3   *The Daily Telegraph*, 10 July 1993

4   *New Musical Express*, 23 August 1963

5   *Melody Maker*, 20 July 1964

6   *New Musical Express*, 2 August 1963

7   *Who's Really Who* by C Miller (Sphere, 1987)

8   *New Musical Express*, 8 February 1964

9   The first British television show to be recorded in colour

10 *Watlington Gazette*, 11 March 1964

11 Quoted in *Beat Merchants* by A Clayson (Blandford, 1996)

12 Titled *Having A Wild Weekend* in the USA

13 *Watlington Gazette*, 11 March 1964

14 *The Guardian*, 11 June 2004

15 *The Guardian*, 31 March 1964

16 *Disc*, 19 May 1964

17 *Daily Mirror*, 3 May 1964

18 *Boyfriend Book 1966* (City Magazines, 1965)

6   Tell The World I Do

1   *The Wit And Wisdom Of Rock And Roll*, ed M Jakubowski (Unwin, 1983)

2   *New Musical Express*, 10 April 1964

3   *Melody Maker*, 23 May 1964

4   *Ready Steady Go* annual, 1965

5   *New Musical Express*, 2 October 1964

6   *Q*, May 1995

7   *Brian Epstein* by R Coleman (Penguin, 1989)

8   *Leader* by G Glitter and L Bradley (Warner, 1992)

9   *Kink* by D Davies (Boxtree, 1996)

10 *She's A Rebel* by GG Garr (Blandford, 1993)

11 *Sunday Times*, 2 May 2004

12 *Playboy*, 19 October 1964

13 *Be My Baby* by R Spector and V Waldron (Pan, 1991)

14 *James Brown* by J Brown and B Tucker (Sidgwick and Jackson, 1987)

15 *Melody Maker*, 12 February 1966

16 *Blue Melody: Tim Buckley Remembered* by L Underwood (Backbeat, 2002)

17 *The Kinks* by J Savage (Faber & Faber, 1984)

18 *Melody Maker*, 7 August 1971

7 Trouble In Mind

1   *Q*, October 1987

2   *Hippie Hippie Shake* by R Neville (Bloomsbury, 1995)

3   *Andover Advertiser*, 2 August 1966

4   *Rock's Wild Things: The Troggs Files* by A Clayson and J Ryan (Helter Skelter, 2000)

5   *Rolling Stone*, 5 November 1987

6   He would also insist that Jagger change 'spend the night' to 'time' in 1967's 'Let's Spend The Night Together'. On the show, Mick rolled his eyes in mock exasperation whenever he sang the doctored line

7   *Melody Maker*, 5 February 1966

8   *The Rolling Stone Interviews*, ed J Wenner *et al* (Straight Arrow, 1974)

9   *Melody Maker*, 5 April 1966

10 *Pop Weekly Annual* ed A Hand (World Distributors, 1965)

11 *New Musical Express*, 16 April 1965

12 *New Musical Express*, 25 June 1965

13 *Rock's Wild Things: The Troggs Files* by A Clayson and J Ryan (Helter Skelter, 2000)

14 *New Musical Express*, 14 January 1967

15 *Zigzag*, May 1973

16 *Wouldn't It Be Nice* by B Wilson and T Gold (Bloomsbury, 1991)

17 *Scott Walker: A Deep Shade Of Blue* by M Watkinson and P Anderson (Virgin, 1994)

18 *Music Echo*, 31 January 1967

19 *Evening Standard*, 23 October 1966

20 *Midland Beat*, No 32, May 1966

21 *Self-Portrait With Friends: The Selected Diaries Of Cecil Beaton, 1926–1974*, ed R Buckle (Book Club, 1979)

22 *Playpower* by R Neville (Jonathan Cape, 1970)

8 Worried Life Blues

1   *The Guardian*, 11 February 2004

2   *The Sun*, 25 January 1983

3   *Oz*, June 1967

4   *The Sun*, 29 June 1967

5   *Sunday Express*, 2 July 1967

6   *Daily Express*, 30 June 1967

7   *Rolling Stone*, 5 November 1987

8   *Daily Mail*, 18 July 1990

9   *Sunday Times*, 10 August 2003

10 Although Jagger's alleged idea of including a picture of himself naked on a crucifix was dropped

11 *Mojo: The Psychedelic Beatles – Special Edition*, 2001

12 *Trend Boyfriend '68 Book* (City Magazines, 1967). This was before 'gay' became a euphemism for 'homosexual'

13 Faithfull had rejected the female lead in The Dave Clark Five's *Catch Us If You Can/Having A Wild Weekend*, considering it 'too poppy'

14 A 1967 Faithfull B-side, 'Tomorrow's Calling' – alias 'Hier Ou Demain' – was an *Anna* opus excluded from the soundtrack album

15 The overseas title of *Girl On A Motorcycle* translated as *Naked Under Leather*

16 *Modern Dating* by Garner Ted Armstrong (Ambassador, 1969)

17 James Fox as 'Chas' in *Performance* (Warner Bros, 1970)

9   The Devil's Shoestring

1   *The Rolling Stone Interviews* (Straight Arrow, 1974)

2   *Time*, June 1970

3   *Who's Really Who* by C Miller (Sphere, 1987)

4   *The Guardian*, 7 July 2004

5   *Village Voice*, September 1968

6   *Inside Classic Rock Tracks* by R Rooksby (Backbeat, 2001)

7   *Faithfull* by M Faithfull and D Dalton (Penguin, 1994)

8   *Rolling Stone*, 5 November 1987

9   *The Guardian*, 11 February 2004

10 *Q*, October 1987

11 *Hippie Hippie Shake* by R Neville (Bloomsbury, 1995)

12 Which provoked the most immediate covers by Merry Clayton (who'd duetted with Jagger on the original) and Grand Funk Railroad. The Stones' own instrumental introit was to resurface in an ITV commercial for an automobile breakdown and relay service

13 *Loose Talk*, compiled by L Botts (Omnibus, 1980)

14 The incident was to be chronicled in 'Altamont' on *666*, the double album by Aphrodite's Child, a Greek combo that was to spawn two solo attractions in Vangelis and Demis Roussos. Don McLean's 1971 hit 'American Pie' would later refer to it more cryptically via allusions to 'Jackflash' and 'no angel born in hell'

10 Take Out Some Insurance

1   *Sunday Times*, 19 August 1975

2   *New Musical Express*, 13 December 1969

3   *Rolling Stone*, January 1970

4   *Melody Maker*, 20 December 1969

5   *Melody Maker*, 1 April 1971

6   *The Times*, 18 July 2003

7   Chris Jagger took charge of Stargroves during his brother's absence in France and elsewhere. Among those who used the Mobile during this period were Led Zeppelin, The Faces and The Who

8   'Cocksucker Blues' was to appear on a bonus single with a Germany-only compilation, *The Best Of The Rest: The Rolling Stones Story* 2, in 1983

9   *The Rolling Stones Chronicle* by M Bonanno (Plexus, 1995)

10 *Hit Men* by F Dannen (Muller, 1990)

11 This concert was broadcast on the late John Peel's *Sunday Concert* in July 1972 and featured a daring new arrangement of 'Satisfaction'

12 *New Yorker*, 5 April 1970

11 Honest I Do

1   *The Rolling Stones Chronicle* by M Bonanno (Plexus, 1995)

2   To Philip Norman

3   Shortly after her confinement, Hunt played 'Bianca' in a production of *Catch My Soul* at the Roundhouse

4   *Sunday Times*, 4 July 2004

5   *Saga*, September 2002

6   *John Winston Lennon* by R Coleman (Sidgwick and Jackson, 1984)

7   *Ink*, June 1971

8   *Hippie Hippie Shake* by R Neville (Bloomsbury, 1995)

9   *The Lamberts* by A Motion (Chatto & Windus, 1986)

10 *Who's Really Who* by C Miller (Sphere, 1987)

11 *Sunday Times*, 23 May 2004

12 *A propos* nothing in particular, 'Ferric Jaggar' was the all-Aryan hero of *The Iron Dream* by Norman Spinrad (Panther, 1972), a contemporaneous novel about a novel by Adolf Hitler recast in a parallel universe as a writer of science fiction

13 With Harry Nilsson on backing vocals and Jack Bruce on bass. A one-sided ten-inch acetate of the result surfaced in 2002, amid much speculation about the high bids it might attract if auctioned

14 Corporately titled 'Exile On Main Street Blues'

15 *Mojo* supplement, undated

16 *Rolling Stone*, 5 November 1987

12 Baby, What You Want Me To Do?

1   *The Rolling Stones In Their Own Words*, ed D Dalton and M Farren (Omnibus, 1980)

2   *Sunday Times*, 4 July 2004

3   *The Rolling Stones Chronicle* by M Bonanno (Plexus, 1995)

4   'He moves like a parody between a majorette girl and Fred Astaire' – *Loose Talk*, compiled by L Botts (Omnibus, 1980)

5   *Chicago Sun-Times*, 20 June 1972

6   Sleeve notes to *The Rolling Stones* (Decca LK 4605, 1964)

7   A sarcastic Jagger named Led Zeppelin's guitarist, Jimmy Page, as one of his three favourite singers in a 1969 *New Musical Express* poll. The others were Yoko Ono and Roger Daltrey

8   The Troggs were to release a remarkable 1975 resurrection of 'Satisfaction'

9   *New Musical Express*, 11 March 1973

10 *Beat Merchants* by A Clayson (Blandford, 1985)

11 *Alias David Bowie* by P and L Gillman (NEL, 1987)

12 *Connection* (German fanzine, autumn 1978)

13 *British Beat* by C May and T Philips (Hamlyn, 1972)

14 *Daily Mail*, 19 July 1990

15 *The Guardian*, 12 May 2004

16 *Leader* by G Glitter and L Bradley (Warner, 1992)

17 I'm not saying there's anything sinister in this, but the engineer for the 'Dancing With Mr D' session became ill with a digestive complaint. Producer Jimmy Miller was also infected, but managed to finish the album. He never worked with the Stones again

18 Because, reputedly, it was composed chiefly by Keith Richards

19 *Serge Gainsbourg: View From The Exterior* by A Clayson (Sanctuary Publishing, 1998)

13 Shame Shame Shame

1   *Woman's Own*, 25 October 1976

2   *Sunday Express*, 1974 (precise date obscured)

3   *The Rolling Stones Chronicle* by M Bonanno (Plexus, 1995)

4   *Rolling Stone*, 6 February 1973

5   *The Trouble With Rock*, CBS News, 11 August 1974

6   In 1988, the same number was the last A-side to date by Dave Berry

7   *NME Rock 'n' Roll Years*, ed J Tobler (BCA, 1992)

8   *The Small Faces & Other Stories* by U Twelker and R Schmitt (Sanctuary Publishing, 2002)

9   *Jeff Beck: Crazy Fingers* by A Carson (Carson, 1998)

10 *National Star*, 19 June 1975

11 *Shattered*, No 20, 26 November 2000

12 1975 interview to Lisa Robinson (quoted in *Shattered*, No 20, 26 November 2000)

13 *The Wit And Wisdom Of Rock And Roll*, ed M Jakubowski (Unwin, 1983)

14 Can't Stand To See You Go

1 *The Rolling Stones Chronicle* by M Bonanno (Plexus, 1995)

2 *Stardust* by T Zanetta and H Edwards (Michael Joseph, 1986)

3 *Soho News* (New York), 9 May 1977

4 *Village Voice*, May 1975

5 Rewritten by Canned Heat as 'Let's Work Together'

6 *Loose Talk*, compiled by L Botts (Omnibus, 1980)

7 *Rock Quotes*, ed J Green (Omnibus, 1977)

8 *Daily Express*, 12 May 1977

9 McLaren was old enough to be remembered by Dick Taylor as a Pretty Things aficionado in 1964, as was Charlie Harper of The UK Subs

10 *Rolling Stone*, 21 August 1980

11 *The Wit And Wisdom Of Rock And Roll* by M Jakubowski (Unwin, 1983)

12 *The Rolling Stones In Their Own Words*, ed D Dalton and M Farren (Omnibus, 1980)

13 *Daily Express*, 14 September 1977

15 Shoot Me, Baby

1 Press conference at Le Beat Route, London, 28 April 1982

2 *Daily Star*, 4 July 1983

3 Revived in the 1980s too by both Sinéad O'Connor and Serge Gainsbourg. See *Death Discs* by A Clayson (Sanctuary Publishing, 1997) for background information on 'Gloomy Sunday', nicknamed 'The Budapest Suicide Song'

4 *The Rolling Stones Chronicle* by M Bonanno (Plexus, 1995)

5 In parenthesis, Jagger also 'owns' almost 2,000 acres of the Moon, having paid a California new-age shop for the deeds

6 *Rolling Stone*, 22 January 1981

7 *Woman's Own*, 21 November 1987

8 *The Sun*, 25 January 1983

9 *Melody Maker*, 2 August 1980

10 *Rolling Stone*, 21 August 1980

11 By Jovan, the perfumiers. This was the first major pop tour to benefit from such input

16 I Ain't Got You

1   *NME Rock 'N' Roll Years*, ed J Tobler (BCA, 1992)

2   *Who's Really Who* by C Miller (Sphere, 1987)

3   *The Times*, 11 April 2004

4   *Sunday Times*, 17 August 2003

5   *Howling At The Moon* by W Yetnikoff and D Ritz (Abacus, 2004)

6   *Q*, May 1995

7   *The Guardian*, 5 December 2003

8   *The Sun*, 27 March 1984. I must add the raw information that, a week after the alleged interview, Wyman denied that it had ever taken place

9   *Rolling Stone*, 5 November 1987

10 *Rolling Stone*, 15 August 1985

11 Jagger with Hall And Oates would be prominent on the soundtrack to the 1986 film comedy *Ruthless People*

12 *The Yardbirds* by A Clayson (Backbeat, 2002)

13 *Jeff Beck: Crazy Fingers* by A Carson (Carson, 1998)

14 The engineer actually took the instruction at face value and wiped it anyway

17 You're Gonna Need My Help

1   *Rolling Stone*, 5 November 1987

2   *Sunday Times*, 17 August 2003

3   *Q*, October 1989

4   *New Musical Express*, 2 September 1989

5   *Q*, October 1987

6   Jagger was to return the compliment four nights later when Turner played at an auditorium in Osaka.

7   *Jeff Beck: Crazy Fingers* by A Carson (Carson, 1998)

8   *Q*, May 1995

9   *Daily Mail*, 19 July 1990

18 My Bitter Seed

1   *Sunday Times*, 1 February 2004

2   *Q*, October 1989

3   *The Guardian*, 27 February 1989

4   *USA Today*, 3 August 1994

5   *Rock 'n' Reel*, No 17, spring 1994

6   *Losing My Virginity* by R Branson (Virgin, 1998)

7   *Sunday Times*, 20 June 2004

8   *The Daily Telegraph*, 1 May 2004

9   *The Times*, 15 November 2003

10 *Sunday Mirror*, 21 March 2004

11 *The Times*, 25 August 2003

12 James Jagger's godmother

13 *The Times*, 13 December 2003

Epilogue: Odds And Ends

1 *Travelling Man* by F Allen (Aureus, 1999)

2 *Sunday Times*, 21 November 2003

Index